THE

STOPPING the TRAIN

STOPPING the
TRAIN

Edwin B. Martin, Jr.

with

Richard N. Côté

CORINTHIAN
BOOKS

Mt. Pleasant, S.C.

Copyright © 2000
Edwin B. Martin, Jr.

Publishers Cataloging-in-Publication Data
(Provided by Quality Books, Inc.)

Martin, Edwin Berry, Jr.
    Stopping the train : the landmark victory over same-sex sexual harassment in the workplace / by Edwin B. Martin, Jr., with Richard N. Côté -- 1st ed.
    p. cm.
    LCCN: 99-65110
    ISBN: 1-929175-08-6

    1. Martin, Edwin Berry--Trials, litigation, etc. 2. Sexual harassment--Law and legislation-- United States. 3. Sexual harassment of men-- Alabama--Birmingham. 4. Sexual abuse victims--Biography. 5. Norfolk Southern Corporation.
    I. Côté, Richard N.

    KF4758.M37 1999   344.01' 25
                         QBI99-1316

Corinthian Books
an imprint of
The Côté Literary Group
P. O. Box 1898
Mt. Pleasant, S. C. 29465-1898
(843) 881-6080
http://www.corinthianbooks.com

To all victims of sexual harassment in the workplace

PREFACE

Most Americans once perceived sexual harassment only as
something that male bosses did to their female subordinates. However, the definition of sexual harassment has
changed radically over the past ten years, especially in the wake
of the U.S. Supreme Court's 1996 ruling on the issue, which is
included under Title VII of the Civil Rights Act of 1964.

Sexual harassment is currently defined as behavior that either
discriminates against an individual because of sex or is so objec-
tively offensive that it alters the victim's conditions of employment. The most obvious type of illegal sexual harassment takes
place when a supervisor requests sexual favors from a subordinate and employment conditions, terms, and benefits depend on
the employee's compliance with the demands.

The second and less demonstrable kind of sexual harassment
occurs when an employee is subjected to a hostile work environment, including sexually explicit or offensive language and or
materials. Sexual harassment can consist of persistent leering or
sexual conversation or more obvious abuse like unwelcome physical contact. The abuse does not have to end in tangible loss, such
as loss of wages or a passed promotion, to be sexual harassment.

The greatest changes in sexual harassment law in the past five
years have been caused by the variety of complaints filed by
victims. For example, conservative estimates claim that men are
filing at least ten percent of all sexual harassment charges and
the numbers are steadily climbing. One reason for this phenom-
enon is that a great number of women have risen to positions of

power in business for the first time in modern history. But not all male victims of sexual harassment accuse women as their attackers. At least half of the harassers are other men.

For several reasons, men have chosen to confront their abusers publicly only recently.

Aside from the fear and pain sexual abuse victims face, male victims of sexual harassment also tend toward feelings of extreme isolation. Often, these men think that no one will believe them or they blame themselves for their inability to end the harassment. They feel that others will view them as less than men because they have lost control over their situations, especially in circumstances where they have been unable to defend their own bodies. The stress of the abuse combined with the self-blame these men feel can be detrimental to their job performance, as well as to their psychological and physical health.

Obviously, it is exceedingly important for employers to be aware of the possibility of same-sex harassment in the workplace and deal with harassment cases in a consistent manner, regardless of gender or status. Employers are ultimately responsible for the actions of their management personnel. In addition to creating a clear grievance procedure for employees, employers should take action against sexual harassment as soon as they become aware of it, stressing the illegality of the behavior. Sexual harassment policy should be distributed to each employee individually and be posted in an accessible and prominent location. Furthermore, employers should consider conducting seminars or workshops to promote company-wide knowledge of the issue.

Not only is such responsible management beneficial for the employees, but it also helps employers avoid expenses due to low productivity, low morale, high employee turnover rates and absenteeism, not to mention steep legal fees.

Not surprisingly, most employers have had no idea how to deal with same-sex harassment claims in the past, although much progress had already been made in curbing male harassment of women and even female harassment of men in the workplace. A man who was harassed by other men could complain to his company's management and nothing would be done. The man's co-workers, witnesses to the harassment, would often dismiss the attacker's behavior as horseplay. The lack of validation from managers and fellow employees undoubtedly contributed to a male victim's feelings of isolation.

Even courts of law could not decide how to treat these cases. Some federal courts held that same-sex harassment is never illegal, while others ruled that it is against the law only if the harasser is homosexual. The case of Joseph Oncale versus Sundowner Offshore Services did much to clarify the matter.

Like the protagonist of this book, Edwin B. Martin, Jr., Joseph Oncale was subjected to sex-related actions and assault by his supervisors and a co-worker. Like those of Eddie Martin, Joseph Oncale's multiple complaints to management were ignored. He felt humiliated in front of his co-workers and feared that his attackers would rape him if he did not quit his job. Eddie Martin's attackers also drove him to quit his job, a fifteen-year railroad career and a multi-generational family tradition. Just as happened to Joseph Oncale, Eddie Martin's charge of sexual harassment was thrown out by a district court because there was no cause of action under Title VII for victims of male-on-male sexual harassment.

Eddie Martin eventually won his case on other grounds, but it wasn't until the Supreme Court's landmark decision in the case of Oncale vs. Sundowner that Eddie actually received any compensation from his former employer. Finally, the Court ruled that all forms of sexual harassment between members of either sex are illegal under Title VII of the Civil Rights Act of 1964. The next day, Norfolk Southern, the railway company for whom Eddie had worked, offered him a financial settlement in compensation for his suffering. Thus Eddie Martin became the first man to benefit tangibly from the Supreme Court's decision that same-sex sexual harassment was both impermissible and actionable under federal law.

Eddie wrote this first-person narrative, *Stopping the Train,* to document his victorious struggle and to inspire others to fight sexual harassment in the workplace. This is the first time a man has spoken out articulately against his harassers after facing the debilitating power of fear and shame same-sex sexual harassment causes.

Eddie's supportive wife, Marcia, whom he met at the beginning of his ordeal, is largely responsible for his survival and recovery as well as his decision to address the subject publicly.

This book clearly explains the course of action that Eddie

Martin took in trying to stop his abuse. It is a familiar story to men in his situation. Although he did all the recommended things to stop the harassment, he was not given the help he deserved. When repeated demands for the behavior to stop caused only escalating attacks from his abusers, Eddie went over the head of his supervisor to management. After he realized the situation was spiraling out of control, he finally began to document the abuse. And when several complaints to management fell on deaf ears, he did the only thing he could. He decided to fight back in court.

In addition to documenting the steps Eddie took in order to prosecute his harassers, *Stopping the Train* also chronicles the stages of Eddie's psychological and physical breakdown, as well as his slow and difficult recovery. Through his chilling accounts, we become witnesses to the outrageous abuse he suffered at the hands of his supervisor and two co-workers. We observe as he becomes a shadow of his former robust self, as fear forces him to withdraw from life, and as his waking nightmare follows him into his dreams. We watch helplessly as Eddie loses the one stabilizing force in his life, his railroad career, and we cheer him on as he begins to build a new life around his love for Marcia and his children.

Eddie Martin's story is ultimately one of triumph over great adversity. In this book, the reader sees him begin to recover, with the help of Marcia and his doctors and lawyers, in the face of humiliation and lies. Eddie's case helped change the policies and training procedures of the business world, and his book may help change them further. Sexual harassment is still a foggy issue for many employers and managers. *Stopping the Train* helps to clarify what constitutes same-sex sexual harassment, what steps need to be taken to end it, and how training can be effective in preventing it. Eddie Martin wants to prevent other victims of sexual harassment from feeling helpless and alone. He hopes that his story will be a comfort to those in need and a useful tool to those in positions to end sexual harassment in the workplace now.

Richard N. Côté
October 30, 1999

1

WORKIN' ON THE RAILROAD

Headaches and heartaches and all kinds of pain
They all ride along with the railroad train.
-Wallace Saunders, "Casey Jones"

Birmingham, Alabama
November 19, 1993
10:30 P.M.

As I walked through the ice-cold railroad yard, it looked like the set from a Stephen King movie. A smoke-like haze blanketed all the buildings and covered the giant General Electric and EMD locomotive engines waiting to be serviced. All that I could make out of the rail cars not more than twenty feet in front of me were coal-black shadows.

I heard the screeching brakes of a train far away. There were no human sounds, only metal on metal. I couldn't hear men calling out to one another. I didn't hear any laughter or conversations. In fact, I couldn't see anyone at all.

The odor of raw diesel fuel in the air made my eyes water and my lungs sting. I could see my breath in front of me. What little light there was came from ancient fluorescent tubes, covered in grease and grime. Their constant buzzing was all around me. The tubes cast an eerie green glow through the haze, like a harbor light in a fog-cloaked inlet. Even my clothes and hands looked green.

I buttoned my jacket and rubbed my hands together. It was

ten-thirty at night and the sky above me was black. Getting a bearing on my surroundings was difficult, if not impossible, since I couldn't see twenty feet in front of me. In a railroad yard, an unobstructed view was essential. I didn't want to be blind-sided by a fast-moving locomotive. In the thick fog, getting hit by an incoming train was entirely possible.

I stepped up the ladder of a four-axle GE electric-diesel engine. The metal railing was cold in my hands and the train was dirty from exhaust. I had always loved standing high above the tracks. I felt some primal power when I looked down on everything around me. With my fingers, I traced the soiled, raised white lettering and horse symbol of the Norfolk Southern logo. Looking around, I saw only the fog.

As I walked up to the yard's fuel pumps and water tanks, I noticed that all of them were covered in thick soot, as if the entire yard had recently survived a fire. Everything around me was timeworn and run-down. The yard looked like it hadn't been updated since World War II. I ran a finger unconsciously across the side of a fuel pump and was surprised at the amount of grease that came off. The place was definitely due for a total overhaul and cleaning.

The maintenance office was as dingy and dirty as the rest of the yard, but a couple of bright fluorescent tubes strung from the overhang cut through the green haze. I thought of the proverbial light at the end of the tunnel as I cast a glance at the darkness behind me.

The well-lit building beckoned me. I wiped my hands on my jeans and walked towards my new office. Heck, I had never seen a yard in worse shape, but it was where I was paid to do the thing I loved: work on trains. I was anxious to get started. It was one of the busiest service yards the railway company ran, and I could hardly wait to get my new job started. As I reached for the doorknob, I couldn't help but wonder what experiences awaited me.

The Norfolk Southern Railroad's Norris diesel shop was located in Irondale, Alabama, a suburb of Birmingham. Although

I was born and raised in the South, the city of Birmingham was foreign to me. I had arrived a couple days earlier and taken a room at the local Sheraton. I left my cat and two dogs in the care of my sister back home in Greenville, South Carolina. It felt funny not having them around my feet every minute of the day.

My hotel room was filled with moving boxes. I had loaded the entire truck bed and passenger seat of my pick-up and hit the road. I brought kitchen supplies, toiletries, winter and summer clothing, golf clubs, a portable stereo, a few paperbacks, and other essentials. None of the boxes were opened. I didn't want to unpack all of my gear, then have to re-pack it when I moved to a more permanent residence.

I had mixed emotions about leaving South Carolina. I had lived there my entire life. At the time, though, I was going through a divorce. I felt better about the break-up since I'd arrived in Birmingham. I didn't enjoy fighting with my estranged wife and I liked even less the necessity of talking through our attorneys.

Still, there was so much to do in South Carolina. I had fond memories of all of the cities I'd worked in and visited. From my home town of Greenville, it was a short couple of hours to Myrtle Beach. Before divorce proceedings with my wife had started, we'd take weekend trips to the seaside city and walk along the boardwalk.

When we were feeling foolish enough, we'd ride on a roller coaster and put off our troubles for a while. But when we got home, things would slowly return to normal and we'd start bickering again. No one likes to see a relationship end. It was even more difficult when you had years of work invested in it. I relished the solitude of the hotel room.

Despite the cramped quarters, hotel life wasn't so bad. There were comfortable beds, the bathrooms had plenty of hot water, and the maid service tidied up the room for me every day. Norfolk Southern provided me with a household expense account for the first month at my new assignment. It was a good deal and I was comfortable, but I couldn't see myself living there for an extended period of time. I preferred having a backyard of my own where I could watch the mourning doves, mockingbirds, squirrels, and other creatures as they went about their daily routines.

A hotel room was not someplace you could call home. Besides, when my kids came to visit, I wanted to give them their own rooms, where they would feel comfortable. I looked forward to barbecuing with my daughter, Micah, and son, Eddie, in a backyard somewhere while the dogs nosed through the underbrush in search of interesting critters. I missed my children already.

On my first day in Birmingham, I went to the maintenance yard for a tour with the master mechanic. I got up that morning at around seven and put on my typical winter "uniform." Working on diesel-electric engines is dirty work. If you wore nice clothes, they were likely to be ruined by shift's end. I pulled on some old jeans, a warm flannel shirt, and a worn pair of steel-toed work boots. I put on a favorite fatigue jacket of mine that I had for years. I needed it that morning.

I was eager to get to work. In South Carolina, I had been in charge of servicing ten to twelve trains per shift. It was enough to keep me busy, but I still had some downtime. The Birmingham facility was a whole other story. Trains from all over the region came into Birmingham. Typically, the yard serviced around twenty-three to twenty-five trains per shift. It was double the work I was used to, but I couldn't wait to give it a go. Because the yard was so busy, I knew that my responsibilities would be greater. I considered it a compliment that Norfolk Southern was giving me the opportunity to show that I was up to the new job.

It took a couple of tries to start my Chevy pickup in the cold morning air. It was about forty degrees outside. I have never liked the cold. The South generally has milder winters, which is one of the reasons I would never leave the area. I was already looking forward to spring, and to sitting on the front porch with my feet propped up. Visitors from the North often can't take the heat and humidity of the South, but I couldn't imagine it any other way.

As I drove through early-morning Birmingham, I was pleased with all of the businesses and industry I saw. Birmingham is located about ninety miles north of Montgomery, Alabama, and 125 miles west of Atlanta, Georgia. It sits roughly in the center of the state. Before moving to the hub of Alabama, I had read about its history. Birmingham had always been an industrial city. As far back as the Civil War, Confederate soldiers constructed a blast furnace there to process the area's rich iron-ore deposits. Shortly after, in 1870, the modern city was founded at the intersection of two newly built railroads. Because of Birmingham's industrial status as the "Pittsburgh of the South," the city had always had close ties with the railroad.

Judging from the bowling alleys, shopping centers, movie theaters, and restaurants, I didn't think I would ever run out of things to do there. I made a mental note to check the phone book for golf courses in the area. I was never a very good golfer, but I sure enjoyed getting out for a relaxing –and sometimes frustrating – eighteen holes with a buddy. Like the bumper sticker said: "A bad day of golf is better than a good day at work."

After stopping for breakfast at a small diner, I asked my waitress for directions to the rail yard. After a few wrong turns and another stop for directions, I finally found it. It was a straight shot to Irondale from downtown Birmingham on Interstate 20. There, I met up with the master mechanic, Tom Bennett. He was in charge of the entire region, which in his case included all of Alabama and parts of Mississippi. I shook hands with Bennett and he welcomed me aboard. He suggested we hop into his company car for the tour.

As we drove around, I realized how massive the yard really was. The Irondale facility was huge. It dwarfed the places I had worked in South Carolina. Miles of tracks separated the stations, which were like small islands connected by rails.

The Norris yard was what's known as a "hump" yard. Trains from all over the region came through at all hours of the day and night. Once there, they were serviced and split up for their next leg of the trip.

If a train from Atlanta came through Birmingham, most of the cars connected were not headed to the same cities. The cars were decoupled one by one and pushed up over a small hump. As the car rolled past the top of the hump, gravity propelled it downhill towards the marshaling yard, an area with over twenty separate tracks. A technician in the tower would then flip switches that would send the car down the correct track, depending on its final destination. As it approached the other cars in a track, a retarder squeezed the car's wheels to slow it down before it rolled into the other cars there and coupled together with them.

Bennett stopped the company sedan at one of many "shacks" – small portable structures where the car inspectors' offices were located. These shacks stood all along the railroad tracks.

We got out and Bennett introduced me to some of the car men, whose job it was to inspect the train cars being pulled by the locomotives. If I serviced twenty-something engines a shift, they had to keep track of a hundred times as many cars.

After brief introductions, I told them that I was going to be working in the locomotive facility at the diesel shop.

"Is he gonna be workin' with Hornbuckle?" asked one of the men, turning to Bennett.

"Sure is," Bennett replied, sending the rest of the men into laughter.

I wondered what this Hornbuckle's story was. I guess I must have had a funny look on my face, because Bennett explained the laughter.

"Yeah, Mr. Hornbuckle is kind of a strange individual." Bennett turned to the car inspectors and said, "He's going to have to learn to work with him."

Then, he made the "so-so" motion with his hand, waddling

it back and forth. The car inspectors nodded their heads in agreement. It seemed this Hornbuckle guy was weird. *No big deal,* I thought. I always gave everyone the benefit of the doubt. After shooting the breeze for a few more minutes, Bennett took me to tour my station: the diesel shop.

Even during the light of day, the diesel shop looked run-down, dirty, and neglected. Bennett pointed out the various areas of the yard. It was a pretty standard layout. Next to the numerous tracks there were water and gasoline tanks for servicing the engines.

I noticed the giant silos filled with sand, which is used to provide the locomotives' metal wheels with better traction. I saw the blue flag warning systems, designed to prevent locomotives from being moved prematurely and possibly harming employees. If there were still technicians working on a locomotive, a flashing blue strobe light was connected to the rail. When the last of the technicians was finished, the mechanical supervisor removed the blue flag.

As a further precaution, derailers were placed on the tracks. If the train began moving before it was ready, it would be derailed. Better a derailed train than a dead worker.

Bennett introduced me to the first shift general foreman, Gerald Benson, his next-in-command. There were general foremen for each of the three shifts, and the first shift general foreman held seniority over his counterparts in shifts two and three. Benson didn't dress like most general foremen on a railroad. He wore nice slacks and a dress shirt, as if to say, "No matter what, I won't be touching a train."

The diesel shop was dirty business, but the foreman wasn't required to dirty his hands while he sat at a computer. Benson seemed to know that. He was cordial enough, if somewhat disinterested in me and my background. I got the feeling he was only being friendly because the big boss was leading me around. Benson acted as though he was counting his days to retirement.

As I looked around, I began to get excited about my new

job. I was starting a new supervisory position. I would have about five men to supervise in one of Norfolk Southern's busiest yards. As the low man on the seniority totem pole, I would be working the third shift. It began at 10:30 P.M. and ended at 7:30 A.M. I didn't care that the yard looked like a war zone or that I would be working the late shift. I was truly in my element whenever or wherever I was working, as long as I was working on the railroad.

So on my first night of work in the Norris shop, after seeing how dark and foggy it got on the yard, I was mentally prepared and looking forward to my new responsibilities. If I did well, I would be rewarded and promoted. It was as simple as that. I opened the door to the office and glanced at my watch. I had arrived a little early for my shift, which I always tried to do. The outside door opened into a tiny room. There was a small desk inside that could be used for paperwork. Crumpled papers and trash were strewn on top of the desk. The floors were covered with mud.

Beyond the front room was the main office. There was very little light in the place. The entire room measured about eight feet by twelve feet. In the middle of the office, taking up most of the open space, was a huge desk with two computers on its surface. To get behind the desk, you had to squeeze by a printer stand. There certainly wasn't a lot of room to maneuver. It was in that office that I would be doing most of my paperwork and work on the computers.

Sitting at the desk was Larry D. Hornbuckle, the "strange individual" Bennett had described earlier. He was about 55 years old and heavy around the middle. He was dressed in dirty overalls and his gray hair was unkempt. When I walked in he was bobbing his head up and down like a chicken strutting around the yard. I would later learn that Hornbuckle was my boss.

As the general foreman for the third shift, Hornbuckle ran the diesel shop from late night to early morning. He had to make sure that all of the paperwork was filed and that his employees were crossing every "t" and dotting every "i." He also had to decide how many engines to place on each train of cars.

With the huge number of trains that came through the Birmingham facility, it was a busy job. It was important we learn to work together as a team. He mostly stayed in the office and worked on the computers, coordinating jobs with other facilities and technicians in other areas of the Norris yard. Looking at Hornbuckle's sloppy appearance, I would never have guessed he was a foreman.

Behind Hornbuckle, leaning up against the back wall in a chair, was Robert "Red" Summerlin. He held the same job I did during second shift. Summerlin wore much the same clothes as I did: old jeans, work boots, and a flannel shirt. He was as tall as I was at about six-foot-two, but he had more muscle and weight. The source of his nickname, his hair was reddish-brown.

Summerlin loved to tell his co-workers about his past as a Navy SEAL. He looked like he had softened a little over the years, but had retained some of the physical condition he had once been in. He also enjoyed bragging about his military days and tour in Vietnam. It was rumored that he had a necklace of human ears, cut from NVA and Viet Cong soldiers. There was something about Summerlin – an almost audible hum, a tension about him. I sensed a dangerous man lurking beneath the surface that I didn't want to disturb.

After seeing the two strangers in the office, I walked over and introduced myself.

"How's it going? My name is Eddie Martin. I'll be working third shift as the mechanical supervisor," I said, extending my hand. I was expecting a polite reply, perhaps a "welcome aboard" or a "good to meet you."

At all of the new yards I had worked throughout my fourteen years with the railroad, I had always been greeted courteously and professionally. Besides, I assumed the man behind the computer was in management. I also expected a brief chat about the office layout and information about job training.

One thing I could always count on with the railroad: it seemed that no matter where I went, if I met another person who worked for the railroad, we were instantly brothers. The railroad business was like a fraternity or the military. Every state had a railroad. I would often bump into railroad people in unlikely places and we'd instantly speak the same language. It didn't matter if I worked in the diesel shop or human resources; the railroad was family.

My outstretched hand was ignored, so I put it back down to my side. Hornbuckle was bobbing his head at me while Summerlin sneered from his chair. About a full minute passed with no one saying anything. *What a couple of strange guys,* I thought. I was waiting for them to break into a smile or offer a friendly greeting.

Instead, Hornbuckle looked right at me and said, "Can I see your dick?"

2

STEAM IN MY BLOOD

I was born in Dixie in a boomer's shack
Just a little shanty by the railroad track
Freight train whistle taught me how to cry
Hummin' of the drivers was my lullaby.
– Roy Acuff, "Freight Train Blues"

The huge F-7 locomotive sped down the railroad tracks, the axles twisting hard to spin the wheels. It was a black beast straight from a childhood nightmare, complete with sharp nose and a single bulging eye in the middle of its face. About a half-mile before the train got to me, the engineer blew the whistle, sounding a shrill scream that could be heard for miles around.

I stood at a crossroads. The railroad warning lights flashed and the bells rang. I barely noticed the warnings. The train looked farther away than it was, but before I knew it, it was right in front of me. In the split-second that it passed, I caught a glimpse of the engineer at the controls. My father's arm slid out of the cab and gave me a wave. He blew the whistle again, just for me, and I grinned from ear to ear.

Mother often used to take my sister, Lynn, my brother, Roger, and me to this railroad crossing outside of Greenville when we were children. There, we would watch my father as he drove train toward North Carolina. I was proud and happy to watch my father guide the huge locomotive and its millions

11

of pounds of cargo down the railroad tracks. It was mind-boggling to know that he was in charge of making sure the giant train reached its destination. It didn't matter to me that he wasn't home much, because I knew he had important work to do. My father, the railroad engineer, was my first hero.

In 1955, I was born into a family that had worked on the railroad since the early 1900s. In the old South, a railroad man was king. Because the railroad paid such good wages and provided handsome benefits, a railroad man was accorded instant respect, especially if he was an engineer.

Both of my grandfathers, two uncles, several cousins, and my father all worked for Southern Railway Corporation. It was a way of life for my family and a good way to make a living, especially for men without a college degree.

Southern Railway's beginnings can be traced back to 1827, when the South Carolina Canal and Rail Road Company was established by the state legislature. Through the years, after many acquisitions and mergers, it became the Southern Railway in 1899. My family was a part of that history and I was proud to be involved.

My mother's father, William "Red" Nesbitt, was also an engineer. He ran The Southern Crescent – now on display at the Smithsonian Institution – and other locomotives between Greenville, South Carolina, and Spencer, North Carolina. This grandfather, who worked for Southern Railway, died shortly before I was born. He witnessed the gradual transition from steam-powered to diesel-electric engines.

My father's father, Clarence Berry Martin, was a car inspector for Southern Railway. He worked in the mechanical department and was in charge of inspecting the cars' brakes. Grandpa Martin was a stickler when it came to safety. He always made sure everything was up to spec before releasing a car for travel, checking the bearings on the wheels and axles for proper lubrication to avoid a "hot box." Without lubrication, the bearings could overheat, seize up, and derail the train. If he found a problem, he would send the cars into the shop for repair. He also died before I was born.

Continuing the family tradition, my father, Edwin Berry Martin, began his career with Southern Railway as a hostler. It was his job to move locomotives in and out of the roundhouse for repairs. A hostler is like an apprentice engineer. Father learned how to operate the locomotives and moved them around the yard. It was only natural, then, that he was eventually promoted to engineer. My father ran the same line that his father-in-law had run between Greenville and Spencer.

I never saw much of my father while I was a child. He was only home about three days a week. As an engineer, he was on call twenty-four hours a day, seven days a week. It was federally mandated that engineers receive eight hours of rest between trips. Once he reached his destination, he would stay in a railroad hotel for eight hours of sleep. After that, he could be called in on a moment's notice. For all practical purposes, he had two homes: Greenville and Spencer.

The railroad inspired complete and utter devotion in its employees. My father was no exception. He felt the railroad was doing him a favor by employing him. He was completely loyal to the company and always willing to give his entire week to his employers. Virtually no one hesitated to go on assignment hundreds of miles away if the railroad called on them, despite obligations to family.

During the unfortunate times when a train derailed, volunteers for the dangerous clean-up assignments were plentiful. Nothing else mattered to these men but their railroad jobs. The railroad life was all they knew and all they could hope for, and that inspired tremendous loyalty.

As a kid, I often found my way down to the Greenville railroad yard. My grandmother lived near the facility. I spent hours watching the huge locomotives rolling into Greenville and setting out for places unknown. I spent hours imagining their exotic destinations and the adventures they would have.

On rare occasions when my father was in town, he sometimes gave me a short ride from one place to another within the rail yard. I was eight years old when my father gave me my first personal tour of a locomotive. Because I was so small, he had to help me up the ladder onto the mammoth machine. My first impression was how incredibly hot it was. With the engine running, it felt like I was standing in the middle of a fire pit.

Dad took me back into the rear of the locomotive where the diesel engine was housed. He showed me all the parts of the engine and how to start it. Then, we went forward into the cab and he pointed out the controls, the throttle, the brake handles, and the air pressure gauges. He allowed me to rev up the engines in neutral. The pitch of the engine was so loud that I fully expected it to lurch forward and throw us both on the floor.

I remember being terrified when we walked out onto the tracks in front of the massive, vibrating engine. I felt the intense heat as it radiated off the locomotive. I was sweating with nervousness. My eight-year-old mind thought: *I need to get the heck out from between these tracks! I don't want to get run over!*

My father didn't talk about many things, but every once in a while, he might tell us a story. There was one time when an automobile had stalled on the tracks. There was no way the train could avoid hitting it. The driver, sensing the inevitable, got out of the car and began running away from it. As the train struck the vehicle, the force propelled the car up and through the air – until it landed right on top of the running driver.

For an impressionable young boy, there were always exciting and gruesome stories floating around the yard about life on the rails. We especially loved the horror stories. There was a dark side to the railroad that wasn't written about in newspapers: many people used trains to commit suicide. It was considered an occupational hazard that as an engineer you would eventually hit someone with a train. A speeding train can require up to half a mile of track before it can come to a stop. Suicidal people often took advantage of that fact and would stand or lay down on the tracks. Some lost souls even set up a lounge chair to await their death.

I remember greeting my father when he came home from a run. He always wore jeans and, depending on the weather, a light shirt or T-shirt. It was in the waning days of steam locomotives, and his clothes were covered from the coal soot that showered over him. Even during the winter, it was hot in the cab of a locomotive. Father never minded the heat, though. Before he became an engineer, he was a railroad fireman. It was the fireman's job to shovel the coal into the furnace that generated the steam. His arms were hard as rocks from shoveling load after load of coal into the fire.

After eighteen years with Southern Railway, my father retired to go into business for himself. Nevertheless, he never lost his love for the railroad. It had faithfully provided meals, clothes, and medical coverage for his family. There still sits in his office a picture of him seated on a giant diesel-electric engine, his smile as wide as the railroad tracks.

I loved being around the railroad. Even at an early age, I saw myself working on it someday. But I was too young to get a job on the tracks. I kept myself busy in other ways while I dreamt of working with trains. I cut lawns around the neighborhood for a dollar. I worked at a Bonanza steakhouse doing dishes and bussing tables. I even sorted mail at the U.S. Post Office.

When I reached my teenage years, the railroad didn't seem as exciting. All I was interested in were cars and girls, in no particular order. I spent my time at Wade Hampton High School studying the mechanics of automobiles and the fairer sex. I got involved in building drag racers and souped-up street cars. Father didn't approve of my wasting time tinkering with car engines. Neither of us knew that I was honing my skills as a train mechanic.

If it was the size of the trains that first attracted me, it was my family's involvement with them over the years that kept me interested. My brother, Roger, never had much interest in

Eddie in his prime, working as a service attendant on the Southern Railroad about 1981.

railroading. Neither did my sister, Lynn, who was a college graduate and trying to make her way in the world of finance. It seemed inevitable that as the middle child, I would one day work for Southern Railway and carry on the family tradition.

After graduating from high school, I attended a technical college for three semesters, but never finished. My heart just wasn't in it. I began working with my father for the next year in his janitorial chemical supply company. Father kept me busy and paid me well, but I knew that the supply business was not for me. During that time, I met my first wife.

In 1979, I was working for my wife's father setting up mobile homes. It was hard work and we were encouraged to get each installation completed as quickly as possible. It took a crew of four of us about three days to set up each home. Then we were on to the next one.

A buddy that I worked with told me that he had just signed on with Southern Railway. It wasn't often that the company was hiring, so I jumped at the chance to put in an application. Besides having better wages and full benefits, I would be fulfilling a childhood dream if I got the job.

I began my life with the railroad on October 10, 1979. At ten dollars an hour, it was more money than I'd ever made in my life. I started out as a service attendant. Much like a full-service gas station attendant, I was responsible for filling the engines' tanks with diesel fuel. I checked the levels of sand, oil, and water, and added them as needed. It wasn't easy work, but I loved it. I felt part of the railroad fabric, connected to over a hundred years of South Carolina railroading. Having never known my grandfathers, the job brought me that much closer to them.

My father never understood me as a younger man. I ran with a wild crowd. After I began work with the railroad, my father saw me in a different light. I went from being an average son to someone he could almost be proud of. When I got a job with Southern Railway, he felt like I'd grown up a little. He began talking to me about my work. He loved to hear any story I had to tell – as long as it had to do with the railroad.

Three years later, I was promoted to roundhouse foreman. As a foreman, I oversaw the work of the service attendants. With the promotion came more responsibilities. I was now in charge of a lot of paperwork and safety issues. Safety was always high on my list of priorities, just as it had been for Grandpa Martin. While I might take risks by walking across railroad tracks or between coupling cars, I always kept an eye out for the safety of my employees. I didn't want anyone's death on my conscience.

Southern Railway was also very conscious of safety. Not only did they want to keep their employees alive, but on-the-job accidents cost the railroads millions of dollars a year. I witnessed many changes over the years in the company's safety procedures. For example, we all used to wear baseball caps around the yard. Then the railroad provided us caps with slogans printed on them, like "Safety First." Later, everyone was issued hard hats.

The railroad kept me moving between yards in South Carolina. Luckily, I was able to stay in Greenville throughout my stay in South Carolina, as all of the yards were an easy commute from my house there. I worked in Greenville, Spartanburg, and Columbia, and I always enjoyed the changes of place and pace.

In 1982, a little over three years after I began working for Southern Railway, the company went the way of its predecessors and merged with another company. Norfolk & Western took over Southern Railway and changed its name to Norfolk Southern Corporation. The railroad more than doubled in size with the merger. Southern Railway had been responsible for numerous firsts in the railroading industry. Its predecessors were the first to carry passengers, military troops, and mail. They were also the first trains to be equipped with lights for night travel. In 1953, Southern Railway was the first to finish the conversion from steam locomotives to diesel engines. When Southern Railway became Norfolk Southern, it was truly the end of an eighty-three-year era.

My wife and I had two beautiful children during my first few years with the railroad. First my daughter Micah was born, and then my son Eddie, who is named after me, came along. Life seemed perfect. I was working in the job I had always dreamed about. I had two wonderful children.

Unfortunately, things between my wife and me were not going well. In 1985, we were divorced and she retained custody of the children.

In October of 1993 I was offered a major promotion: to mechanical supervisor. I felt like I was really going places in the company. I had worked hard for the railroad for fourteen years.

There was only one problem: I had to transfer to another state because of corporate downsizing. Norfolk Southern was eliminating many overlapping jobs in South Carolina. Apparently, there were already too many mechanical supervisors in

Eddie's two children, Eddie and Micah, were proud that their dad was a "railroad man."

the state. That meant I would have to move from my lifelong home.

My Norfolk Southern supervisors took me aside and handed

me a list. On it were the names of five cities: Kansas City, St. Louis, Roanoke, Danville, and Birmingham. They told me that I could choose where I wanted to be transferred. I decided to make a few calls before making my choice. If I was going to be moving to parts unknown, I knew that I had to look into each city in turn.

Right off the bat, I dismissed Kansas City and St. Louis. Missouri seemed too far north and prone to colder temperatures in the winter. For that same reason, I eliminated Danville, Kentucky. I just didn't like it when the temperature dipped to freezing. At least in the South, the climate was mild year round – except for the summers – and snow was almost non-existent.

That left Roanoke, Virginia, and Birmingham, Alabama, both southern stations. As far as I was concerned, the South had the friendliest people of any region. It was a part of the country that was wholly unique.

Roanoke was nestled in the middle of Virginia and the drive from Greenville wasn't too long. It was the nerve center of Norfolk Southern Corporation and promised to be a busy station. Birmingham was a huge facility and also very busy. It was close to my home in South Carolina, too.

I made a few phone calls to the diesel shops in both Roanoke and Birmingham. In my experience, talking to the men who worked in the facility was better than listening to upper management. I liked to go straight to the source. I talked to mechanical supervisors in both cities to get their perspectives. If anyone was an expert on the way things were run in a particular station, it was the mechanical supervisors.

Birmingham began to sound more and more appealing. I talked to Red Summerlin on the phone from Greenville and he told me how things were run in the Birmingham shop. It was very busy, he said. It had state-of-the-art equipment. There was a great group of employees. And I knew the city itself was large and offered any number of things to do.

I was excited when I told Norfolk Southern that I had decided on Birmingham. I filled out the transfer paperwork and signed a pile of forms forms. I said my good-byes to fellow employees at the Greenville yard, which was hard to do. I had worked with many of the men for most of my fourteen years at the railroad. It was like leaving a family behind.

When I told my children that I had to be moving away for a while, they took it hard. I explained to them that I would come home for Christmas and would try to see them on their birthdays. As difficult as it was to be moving away, it was made even harder by Norfolk Southern's tight schedule: I had two weeks to get my affairs in order and move to Birmingham.

3

THE DIESEL SHOP OF HORRORS

Birmingham, Alabama
November 1993

T he hair on the back of my neck actually stood on end. I thought Larry Hornbuckle had to be joking when he asked to see my penis. What the heck kind of greeting was that from one railroad man to another? I had never met the guy. I didn't know him from Adam and had nothing against him. I smiled nervously as I waited for the punch line. The trouble was, there wasn't one coming.

When I told him, "No, you can't," I expected the gag to be over.

Instead, Hornbuckle asked, "Well, would you like to see mine?"

Again, I answered no. I felt my face flush and my smile vanish. I was no prude, but then again no man had ever asked to see my penis. Neither had I ever been offered a look at someone else's.

Summerlin remained leaning back in the chair against the wall, grinning at the conversation.

I thought, *this must be some type of hazing ritual. They probably do it to all the new guys.*

We held our positions for another full minute; Hornbuckle bobbed his head up and down, Summerlin leaned against the wall, and I stood facing them both. I wouldn't have been surprised if Rod Serling had popped out from behind the door and given an introduction to a *Twilight Zone* episode. Just when I thought that things couldn't be more uncomfortable, it was business as usual.

"I'm Larry Hornbuckle, the general foreman for third shift. That's Red Summerlin, mechanical supervisor for second shift." I nodded my head but didn't offer them my hand again. Neither did they offer theirs.

I listened as Hornbuckle outlined what my next few weeks would be like. He told me that I would be training with a man named Cheatham. I was relieved by that time. I could talk about servicing trains. It was a great relief from being forced to fend off sexual advances from a man.

I enjoyed the bustling Norris diesel shop. The busy nights seemed to make the time move that much faster. Before I knew it, the sun would rise and it would be time to go home. It was different back in Greenville. There, you sat around waiting for a train to arrive so that you could work on it. At the Birmingham yard, there was no such thing as downtime. When you were on shift, you were working. If you didn't, you fell behind.

I supervised many good men on the third shift. I knew that their job often got monotonous. Most of them had been at the yard for some time, so I found it helpful to ask them about procedures at the Norris shop. They knew where everything was located and which trains had higher priority at this particular yard. As a supervisor, I knew it was important to involve employees in the decision-making process.

Curtis Brierly was a hard-working service attendant who had been with Norfolk Southern for five years. He was supporting a family and the late hours were hard on him. Curtis never complained, though. When I asked him to perform some basic task or check somebody else's work, he never said a word in complaint. He knew what he was doing. Curtis was a good person to talk to while I got the job done.

Al Bradford, Jerry Dagnan, Charlie Rice, and Tom Burgay also worked for me. Al and Jerry were quiet men who kept to themselves. They knew their jobs and did them well. Charlie needed a little more supervision in order to get his work done. Sometimes, I'd catch him sleeping. That was dangerous in the service department. A man might lose an arm or leg if he wasn't paying attention.

Tom Burgay was a nice enough fellow. Most of the conversations I had with Tom involved his personal religious convictions. He was known around the yard as a "Bible-thumper," and any words out of his mouth centered on "the glory of God." Like me, he didn't appreciate foul language on the job, especially when it was directed at him.

That first week was a busy one. I was getting to know my job and the men who worked for me. I had to learn the layout of the yard. Because Birmingham was twice as busy as Greenville, I had to train myself to do my job a little quicker than I was accustomed to. With over twenty trains coming in each shift, there was no slack time.

The week was filled with training. The first-shift general foreman, Gerald Benson, assigned an instructor to me. The first-shift mechanical supervisor, Cheatham, told me what was required of me and showed me the paperwork that needed to be filled out.

We went over payroll procedures, which I was already familiar with. But I noticed that Cheatham didn't go over the safety procedures, which surprised me. It was important to review safety procedures with new employees, especially at such a heavily trafficked yard.

Cheatham also informed me that he wasn't very fond of Hornbuckle. I told him I really didn't know the man and couldn't judge him. But in that first week of work, I had the opportunity to observe my new boss. It wasn't so much what he said, though he seemed to have a problem with everyone but Summerlin and Preston "Thad" Thomasson, a third-shift service attendant. Part of it had to do with Hornbuckle's mannerisms and his speech. In my peripheral vision, I often caught him staring at me, and Hornbuckle couldn't let one sentence go by without inserting "fuck" or "shit" or "asshole."

Of course, Hornbuckle and Summerlin had something to say about everything that my first-shift counterpart was teaching me. According to them, he didn't know up from down. They began telling me not to listen to what Cheatham said, and only to do what they said. Finally, Summerlin went to the first-shift general foreman and complained about Cheatham's teaching abilities. I guess he must have been convincing, because Summerlin became my new teacher.

During the second week, Summerlin told me the opposite of everything my former trainer had taught me. He taught me how to fill out the paperwork efficiently, but that was all the help he provided. Summerlin thought he was the ultimate authority. When we received "consists" from Atlanta telling us which locomotives to put with which trains, he often ignored the instructions.

"These guys are full of shit. We're not gonna do it like that," he said. Then he made up his own orders. "This one's got to go here, this one there. If they don't like it, the hell with them."

Summerlin had no authority to change company orders, but he did it anyway. I couldn't help thinking, if this is the way he acted in Vietnam, it's a wonder he made it out alive.

A week into my job I realized I hadn't once thought about my divorce proceedings since I started. That was a relief. Before I left South Carolina, I had thought of little else. It was the little things back home that used to spark the memories of my wife: a restaurant we used to frequent, the park, a woman's profile. Now, I was only thinking about my new duties and responsibilities. There was so much to do.

I was starting to like Birmingham. It was the largest place I had ever lived in. Birmingham housed five times as many people as Greenville. On my off time, I drove through the city and looked around. I even found time to go to the movies and see *Jurassic Park.* The University of Alabama at Birmingham was large and impressive, hard to imagine in a city so immersed in industrial businesses. I always regretted not finishing college.

I was happy that Norfolk Southern hadn't transferred me up North, because I knew I could never be happy outside of the South. I loved the temperate climate. I enjoyed the friendliness of the people. I felt connected to the land as only someone from the South can. I admired the self-reliance of the people and their stubborn refusal to stay down.

I wasn't worried about my move to a city where I knew no one. I had always made friends easily. People told me that I had a likeable personality. Whatever it was, I was always eager to meet new people. I was beginning to crave a simple, friendly conversation. Besides, golfing was more enjoyable when you had a friend to complain to when you hooked a shot into a bunker.

I wasn't really worried about my new job, either. I had fifteen years' seniority with the railroad. I had never had any trouble with new responsibilities. If anything, the more responsibilities I had, the happier I was. I loved a challenge. If a train came in and it had a problem that none of my technicians could figure out, I enjoyed putting my knowledge to the test. I knew the diesel-electric engines I serviced as well as I did the go-karts I tinkered with in my youth. When I was presented with a problem, I found a solution.

I was always a hard worker. Even before my job with the railroad, I can't remember a time that I wasn't working at one job or another. In the South, men grew up quickly and went to work. My parents admired a strong work ethic, so I got my first job when I was fourteen.

As far as I was concerned, my rocky start in the Norris diesel shop didn't mean anything. Every day I learned a little more about the job and how to do it better. I never had doubts about my abilities. It might take a little time, but I knew I would get a handle on things. I only wished that my supervisor and counterpart would help me more with the transition.

Rumors flourished in the railroad business. If there was to be a new policy, employees often knew about it months before it was implemented. So it was not unusual that I had heard about Bill Goggins, the man who was expected to get the job of mechanical supervisor instead of me. He was a friend of Hornbuckle, Summerlin, and Thomasson. They had all wanted and expected Goggins to get my job. After all, they reasoned, he had been filling in as mechanical supervisor for the past year or so before I had moved in. As absorbed in my job as I was, I wasn't paying much attention to the rumors.

Still, I knew I was a source of frustration for these three men. Never mind the fact that I had not promoted myself, nor had I been in charge of moving Goggins elsewhere.

Hornbuckle, Summerlin, and Thomasson were angry that their buddy wouldn't be around any more. In their eyes, I was the reason. I was on the receiving end of some harsh stares my first couple of days at the yard. Often, I would see the men huddled together, whispering like women at a club social. Whenever I walked near, they'd stop their conversation abruptly and stare silently at me.

There were other things about the three men that put me on edge. Hornbuckle was like a schoolyard bully, the kind who speaks with his body. Thomasson had the traits of a gang member. He would follow the bully anywhere – even into violence. Summerlin reminded me of any number of Vietnam vets who, unfortunately, couldn't leave the past behind; they spent their lives seeking out their own wars.

As I'd once heard on *The Shadow,* a radio crime drama, "Who knows what evil lurks in the hearts of men?" I was about to find out at the hands of Larry Hornbuckle, Red Summerlin, and Thad Thomasson.

Thad Thomasson was younger than I. He worked for me two or three nights a week on the third shift. He had greasy red hair that he kept in a ponytail. His full beard was always unkempt. It grew where it wanted to grow: three inches long in some places, bald in others. He wore a black leather jacket and concealed a folding knife in a sheath on his belt. If appearances count for anything, he looked rough, like a member of Hell's Angels.

His clothing was filthy, too. At the railroad, we wore clothes that we didn't mind getting dirty. We washed our clothes on a regular basis, though. Thomasson looked like he'd worn the same outfit for a month straight. There was grease and soot caked on his jeans and shirt. His hands were perpetually stained with grease. His fingernails, long and yellow, were packed with dirt. It seemed like his off time was spent working on automobiles or motorcycles, and he didn't bother to wash up before his shift at the yard. His vocabulary, like his appearance, was filthy.

As a mechanical supervisor, I was in charge of coordinating the servicing of every diesel locomotive that came into the shop. If there were any mechanical problems with them, Hornbuckle had to decide what we were going to do: fix the locomotive or replace it with another. He did most of the paperwork, and I did all the physical work.

He began giving me false information about my job. He'd say, "We've got to put these engines together on that track." I'd go get the men together and we'd do what he told me. Then, I'd walk back in the office and he'd say sarcastically, "Shoot, I'm sorry. I made a mistake. We've got to switch all those engines around again." Then, he'd flash me a crooked grin.

Hornbuckle relished making me look bad. The men began wondering if I knew my job. He was giving me false orders on a regular basis, and I was powerless to stop him. He was, after all, my boss. When he told me to perform a task in a certain way, I had to do it or risk getting fired for insubordination.

Hornbuckle never tried to help me learn the job. He left me in a sink-or-swim situation. I had worked in the railroad industry for fifteen years, but not in this capacity. The Norris yard was a fast-paced environment and we had to do a lot of work to keep the trains moving. I'd go outside with the servicemen and try to figure out what they were doing, what trains they were building. I also tried to be in the office so I could figure out what Hornbuckle based his decisions on. He left me in the dark. When I had questions about the decisions he'd made, he never answered them.

I was relying on instinct and common sense in an attempt to do my job. I began keeping visual track of which trains came in and the order in which they'd arrived. Then, I'd put my men to work. We'd begin fueling and watering the trains that were needed first. At times it felt like there were ten engines arriving on top of each other. I told myself, don't get rattled. You've done this work for years. Just take a deep breath and set a pace for yourself.

I began to get a feel for the job, despite Hornbuckle's attempts at sabotage. I relied more on the paperwork than his verbal commands. It was the only thing I could do if I wanted to keep up with the locomotive traffic. If Hornbuckle had a problem with the way I was doing things, I could always point out the company orders that were coming off the printers. At shift's end, it felt good to look back on a full, successful night's work.

I tried to discipline some of the employees on several occasions. When I disciplined a union man, I always tried to have a higher-ranking witness. Also, I never wanted to pick somebody in the same union as the man I was trying to discipline. Fellow union members never ratted each other out. I would need Hornbuckle if I wanted to discipline somebody properly and I knew he would never help me by witnessing the reprimand.

There was one time that I couldn't raise a couple of my men on the radio. I finally found them asleep in the locker room, a severe infraction. I went to Hornbuckle and said, "They're in there sleeping and I'm tired of having to hunt 'em down. Let's get this handled, get it taken care of."

Hornbuckle didn't say a word. He didn't even bother getting out of his chair. It was like I didn't exist. Looking back, that might have been preferable.

The first time Hornbuckle physically touched me was when Summerlin was teaching me the paperwork end of the job. I filled out the federal paperwork when a locomotive was finished. The service schedule for each engine was printed out on the office printer. If an engine's wheels needed to be checked or the bearings lubricated, it would be on the printout. In order to get to the printer, I literally had to wedge myself between the desk and printer stand. Sitting behind the desk, as always, was Larry Hornbuckle.

Summerlin told me to go and retrieve the latest orders from the printer. When I walked in the office Hornbuckle had his feet propped up on the desk, a common pose for him. I squeezed over to the printer. As I was tearing off the sheet of paper, I felt a hand grab my buttocks firmly. I did what any normal person would do in a similar situation: I jumped and yelled. Pushing past the printer, I turned around and glared at Hornbuckle. He was smiling like a hog in mud.

"What the heck was that about?" I asked him, feeling the anger creep into my throat. The man had been ignoring me for the past two weeks. He had attempted to make me the fool in front of my subordinates. Now, he was grabbing my rear.

"I don't know what you're talkin' 'bout," he replied, his smile replaced by a cold stare.

I left the office quickly and purposefully. I remembered pinching a few buttocks as a child. When I used to do it, at eight or nine years old, I only pinched girls. I had grown out of it. I didn't know what Hornbuckle's problem was. All I knew was that I was going to have to keep a closer eye on him.

After that first confrontation, Hornbuckle and Thomasson must have declared open season on me. Every time I turned around, one of them would be behind me. There, in the dimly lit office, these two men assaulted me physically and verbally. They were merciless and unstoppable. Summerlin never joined in on the physical assaults, but he was often present for them. He thought his buddies were hilarious.

Hornbuckle's seat behind the desk gave him pole position for reaching me. Every night that I worked with him, on every occasion that I retrieved the printouts from the office, he grabbed at my rear end or my genitals. There was nothing that I could do or say to make him stop. I yelled at him. I pleaded with him, but he was unrelenting in his attacks. He would pinch the back of my leg and rear so hard that he would bruise the skin. Looking in the mirror at home, my backside was covered with black and blue marks.

He did not grab me in a joking manner. There were no smiles or laughs from him. He wanted to assert himself over me physically. What made it worse was his being a man. In my experience, men do not grab other men on the butt and crotch. Having played high school sports, I was familiar with the "football pat." After doing well on the field, you might get a friendly pat on the rear from a teammate to acknowledge your good play. It was not prolonged or malicious – and definitely not sexual. But this was a diesel engine maintenance shop, not a high school football team. We were a group of professional mechanics with jobs to do. I seemed to be the only professional there.

Besides using "fuck" and "shit" every other word, Hornbuckle was always ready with a rude comment. Curtis Brierly, Jerry Dagnan, and I were all fairly thin. Hornbuckle picked up on this and begin to tell us that we all looked like we had AIDS. I didn't consider a joke about the deadly disease a laughing matter, but Hornbuckle apparently did. He took to calling us the "AIDS Three" to our faces and in front of others.

I would often see written into the dirt on the side of a locomotive: "Eddie Loves Men." However, since Hornbuckle hardly ever left the office, I assumed either Summerlin or Thomasson had written it.

But that wasn't enough for Hornbuckle. He also began calling Brierly, Dagnan, and me the "Three Muske-Queers." This would send him into hysterics. He hurled these insults at us throughout our shift and referred to us by these names when he talked to others. He would say things like, "Yeah, I got the Three Muske-Queers working tonight."

Thomasson, a subordinate of mine, began participating in the harassment. Because Thomasson and Hornbuckle were friends, I felt my authority over my subordinate slip through my fingers. He and Hornbuckle would take turns pinching my rear. I was miserable. I felt like I had lost control of the situation. The arms coming at me from every direction made me feel like there was a horny octopus in the office with me. I would often have to leave the room for fear of losing my temper.

Thomasson also made "kissy" faces at me, puckering up his lips and lunging towards me. He cornered me in the office and walked right towards me, pursing his lips and making smooching noises. I'd tell him, "Get the heck away from me!" He wouldn't listen and kept coming.

"Cut this crap out!" I said forcefully on more than one occasion, as subtly as a runaway locomotive. "This is not right!" If I had punched Hornbuckle like I wanted to, I would have been fired from my job. The railroad was all I had at the time. I needed that job and I wasn't going to let anybody take it away from me. I still figured that I could talk to Hornbuckle about what he and Thomasson were doing. I didn't realize that they were not capable of reason.

Thomasson was out of control, but Hornbuckle began harassing me every chance he got. He wouldn't listen to any of my protests, and I was rendered powerless as a supervisor because I didn't have anybody to back me up. I attempted to talk to Hornbuckle, telling him, "Listen. You two have got to leave me alone. I can't do my job with you guys pulling this crap. Back off." Hornbuckle would only sneer at me like I was something he'd just scraped off his shoe.

For the life of me, I couldn't understand any of this behavior. I wracked my brain, thinking maybe I said something when I first met them that they took the wrong way. Try as I might, I couldn't think of anything I'd done or said to them. Their attacks were totally unwarranted. As my shifts came and went, I spent the time trying to protect myself from the physical assaults and turning a deaf ear to their insults.

If I was suffering, so was my job. I began neglecting my obligations. I'd fail to fill out the necessary paperwork. I would get behind and forget to direct my servicemen in their duties. Engines began sitting longer than necessary before being serviced.

For the first time in my life, I dreaded going to work. I used to look forward to servicing the trains and couldn't wait to get to the yard. But now, my mind was completely occupied by the fear of continued harassment. Before I knew it, a month had passed at the diesel shop. I could think of nothing but the grabbing, the pinching, the taunts, and the insults. Memories of the mammoth locomotives and the joy I once received from working on them vanished. On my way to and from work, visions of Hornbuckle and Thomasson played through my mind. I saw their movements at home while trying to watch television or lying awake in bed.

They never let up. They were the Energizer Bunnies from Hell. If Hornbuckle wasn't goosing me while I was at the printer, Thomasson was pinching my thigh. Whenever I thought that things couldn't get any worse, they did. It would have been bad enough with Hornbuckle and Thomasson calling me names and grabbing me in uncomfortable places. Little did I know that these men were only warming up.

4

A BREATH OF FRESH AIR

Hear that lonesome whippoorwill?
He sounds too blue to fly.
The midnight train is whining low,
I'm so lonesome I could cry.
–Hank Williams

Birmingham, Alabama
January 1994

I was falling fast without any emotional net. I knew that I couldn't continue to face these horrors alone. I needed some one to talk to, and my parents were not an option. I could hear my father telling me to "just deal with it" or "tell them to stop." I couldn't blame him, though. What I was going through was not a common grievance on the railroad. In all of my fourteen years with the railroad, I had never heard of a man sexually harassing another man. I didn't know anyone who had gone through what I was living every day.

My divorce had battered my self-esteem. The harassment at work was taking its toll on me, too. I didn't want to socialize with anyone. Crowds were beginning to make me edgy, and I was nervous all the time. I was in no condition to go out on the dating scene, but I was starved for human contact. I was in a city where I knew no one. My closest friends were all in Greenville. I was lonely and desperately needed someone to talk to.

I had always scoffed at the commercials I saw on television

that advertised dating services. Who needed a service to find a date? I thought that it was only for losers, people who were ugly and couldn't possibly find anyone by themselves. But as I sank lower and lower into depression, a dating service sounded more and more appealing. It was easy to use and I could look over the personal profiles and photos of many single women. I opened up the yellow pages and browsed the advertisements. Then I picked out an agency that was nearby and called them up.

Hesitantly, I entered the dating service office and looked around. I couldn't believe that I was about to sign up, but I went for broke and sat down. The man who ran the service told me how it worked, and offered me a notebook containing the basic information on the women who were listed with his agency. Each profile outlined the woman's vital statistics, including occupation, likes, dislikes, hair color, and height. No names, addresses, or phone numbers were listed. The proprietor told me that when I found a woman who seemed appealing, then I could view her video.

I was flipping through the notebook half-heartedly when the smiling face in one photo caught my eye. Marcia Maxwell gazed back at me from the page. She had blonde hair and a radiant smile. As I read her profile, I became more and more intrigued. It seemed that, like me, she was new to Birmingham and didn't know anyone. Before telling the proprietor I was ready, I hurriedly picked out two more profiles.

The next step was the video screening. I watched the first two video profiles with disinterest. Then, it was time for Marcia's video. As soon as I heard her voice, I knew that she was the one. Marcia was happy and bubbly, and she seemed to be a fun-loving woman. She was beautiful and intelligent. I knew for certain that Marcia was somebody that I wanted to be around. Despite my apprehensions, I thought, *What the heck, I'm gonna give it a shot.*

I told the proprietor that I had made my choice. He had me fill out a profile for myself and answer a few standard questions on video. I paid him the fee and left. The next day, he said, he would call Marcia and tell her a little about me. If she liked what she heard and wanted me to call her, the proprietor would give me her phone number so that I could talk to her directly. I spent a nervous night hoping that she would find me interesting enough to talk to.

Soon I got the good news. Marcia was willing to talk to me. When I received the green light to call her, I gave some careful thought about how to go about it and what to say. I didn't want to mess up this conversation. I was nervous. Very nervous!

When we talked for the first time, we hit it off almost immediately. There were no uncomfortable silences or lapses in conversation. It felt very natural. We talked for over an hour. Marcia had just moved to the Birmingham area from Albertville, Alabama, about an hour and a half to the northeast. She didn't know much about Birmingham, but had been to a few of the historic sights. It seemed that we had both been unlucky in previous relationships. She had been divorced two months earlier.

Marcia was originally from Texas and had a heart as big as the state. Her outlook on life was unique and fresh. She maintained a "never-say-die" outlook, despite the problems she had encountered in the past. I wished I could be half as positive as she was. Marcia had dreamed about finding her true love since she was a little girl. But, like me, she had been very disappointed by love.

I could relate to what she had been through. Though I had never been in an abusive relationship, I was familiar with the disappointment you felt when you knew your marriage was failing. We spoke the same language, and it felt nice to share our similar backgrounds. She was easy to talk to and had an infectious laugh. I loved to hear her giggle.

Marcia had signed up with the video dating service on a whim. She didn't place much stock in their abilities, but figured, if nothing else, she would have control over her potential suitors. She had been on a few dates after her divorce, but found the men overbearing and too headstrong. Now, the service would help with the screening process. She was always free to reject anyone she wasn't interested in. I was thankful that she hadn't rejected me.

When the service called Marcia and told her that I was interested in speaking with her, she was apprehensive. She hadn't had any luck in the past couple of weeks. After hearing about me and my job, she became interested in getting to know me. She knew that I had two children I adored and that I was a hard worker. Without the benefit of seeing my photo or watching my video, she agreed to let me call her.

At the end of that first conversation, I told Marcia that I'd like to take her to dinner. She asked me when, so I bit the bullet and said, "What about this evening?"

She laughed and said that would be fine. Because I didn't know my way around the city, she gave me directions to a Sam's Wholesale Club and we agreed to meet in the parking lot. I was very nervous about our face-to-face meeting and spent the rest of the afternoon combing my hair and trying on different shirts.

When I pulled into the parking lot at 6:30, I was surprised to see that she and I drove the same pick-up truck: a maroon Chevy S-10. I pulled up beside her and got out. She had a big smile on her face when she got out of her truck. She looked beautiful. She was wearing a catsuit with a Santa Fe print, a long skirt, and a crocheted sweater. Because the temperature was in the thirties, we each wore a coat. I nervously shook her hand.

I had invited her to dinner, but I had absolutely no idea where to go. Maybe Marcia sensed this, because she immediately took control of the date. She knew a little about the historic areas and wanted to show me around before dinner. Because she was having trouble with her truck, I let her drive mine. She told me that we were going to see the statue of Vulcan, the mythological god of metalworking and fire, who was the blacksmith of the gods.

Vulcan Park sits high atop Red Mountain. Cast from iron and standing 55 feet tall, the statue overlooks Birmingham, commemorating the city's history in the iron industry. He is also a safety reminder. In his outstretched hand is a torch, which is lit with a green light. When there is an automobile fatality, the torch turns red as a reminder to drive carefully.

As we slowly rode the elevator up to the top of the tall observation deck, I began to feel queasy. I had never suffered from a fear of heights. But when Marcia and I rode the elevator, I wasn't thinking of the height. I was nervous and trying hard not to bump into her. Suddenly, I had a panic attack.

For no obvious reason, I became extremely frightened. I latched onto the rails in the elevator and had a feeling of imminent death, like something was getting ready to kill me. I began sweating and having hot flashes. My breath was shallow, and I felt like I wasn't getting enough oxygen. I was in a cage and fighting for my life. There were no rational thoughts going through my mind. All I could think about was getting out of the elevator.

The entire episode lasted only about thirty seconds. When we got to the top and out of the elevator where I could walk around, I began to feel better. Marcia asked me if I was all right. I shrugged it off and tried to pretend that nothing had happened. She let it slide.

At the top of Vulcan is a circular room with glass windows all around. As we looked outside, the city lights of Birmingham below me brought me back to reality. I realized where I was and who was with me. We looked out across the city and into the cool, clear night. She took my hand in hers and we held hands. It felt wonderful.

I pointed out the Irondale yard where I worked. She pointed in the direction of the suburb where she lived. After about fifteen minutes, we decided to go to dinner. She suggested Chili's restaurant. I didn't have much of an appetite, but I resolved not to spoil the evening by complaining. My lack of appetite was due partly to my nervousness over our first date, but more of it had to do with work. I picked at the flowering onion appetizer that came but didn't order any dinner. Marcia ordered a hamburger and, like a good Southern woman, tried to get me to eat a little something.

We talked throughout dinner. I told Marcia about my children visiting the previous weekend. She asked lots of questions about them. She sensed how much I loved them and how proud of them I was. I never needed much prompting to talk about my kids. They were the joy of my life. Marcia gave me her undivided attention.

We also talked about my job. I wasn't comfortable talking about Birmingham, so I stuck with safer memories from Greenville and Spartanburg. I told her about my duties and some of the men I had worked with. I knew I needed someone to talk to about the Norris diesel shop, but now was not the time. I hoped I wasn't boring her, but she didn't seem the least bit disinterested.

Despite my nervousness, she quickly put me at ease with her sense of humor and warmth. When she got up to use the restroom, I took a long look at her catsuit. I was thankful that as a man I would never have to wear anything that difficult to get on and off. Before I thought about it, I told her, "I'd love to see you get out of that thing!"

Marcia gave me a strange look before it dawned on me that what I'd said sounded like a line. I blushed.

"I didn't mean that. I just meant that it must be hard to—"

"It's okay, Eddie. I'm just teasing you," she said. Later, she told me that she thought I might be a weirdo after I made that comment.

The night was cut short because I had to work at eleven. We drove back to Sam's and got out of my truck. I didn't want to see her go. I sure didn't want to go to work. Just thinking about Hornbuckle and Thomasson coming after me was enough to make me sweat.

Marcia and I stood around awkwardly for a couple moments

before she again took control. Leaning in close to me – she smelled wonderful – she gave me a perfect, gentle kiss. We said goodnight and I promised to call her the next evening.

The next day, Marcia called me. I was happy knowing that she was genuinely interested in me. Over the next few days, we talked on the phone quite a lot. It seemed like Marcia and I had known each other our entire lives. She was always cheerful on the phone and full of life. I couldn't help but be infected by her cheerful disposition. For the first time in a long time, I felt alive.

Marcia was working as a hygienist in Birmingham, but she lived in the suburb of Gardendale. On one of my days off, she called me from work. She knew how lonely I was, especially living in a hotel room. All I seemed to do was lie in bed and half-watch the television. She asked me to ride out to Gardendale with her so she could show me where she lived. She said she had to let the dog out and change out of her scrubs from work. Then, we could go get something to eat. I agreed to go.

When we got to her house, she introduced me to one of her best friends: her dog. She told me that if I didn't get along with her dog, it would never work out between us. Luckily for both of us, I love animals. Marcia watched me getting along with her friend and smiled. After she changed out of her work clothes, we sat on the couch. There was almost an audible click in the room, and before I knew it, we were kissing like a couple of lovesick teenagers. It was afterwards that things between us really progressed, and we knew we had each found somebody special. Together, we seemed to make sense.

That night, right before we went to dinner, I had another panic attack in her hallway. Besides the sweating and rapid heart rate, many irrational thoughts crept through my mind. I had paranoid visions of the police coming after me. I saw people laughing and staring at me for things that had happened at work. In my mind, total strangers began blaming the harassment on me. My face went pale and I had to lie down on her bed for ten minutes. Marcia was very polite and didn't pry. I could tell that she was worried though.

The time I spent with Marcia was like a vacation from my problems. She told me that she felt safe with me. Slowly, I began to tell her about the things that had been going on at work. I gave her little snapshots of the harassment imposed on me by my boss and his buddy. She listened quietly to everything I told her. I had tons of baggage I needed to unload, and she seemed willing to bear the weight.

When I found it too difficult to go on, Marcia stopped me and held me in her arms. Because of the anxiety I was experiencing, our relationship was unlike any other I'd had. I didn't like to go out in places where there were large crowds or too much noise. All I wanted to do was stay inside and sit with Marcia. She never blamed me for my anxieties. She was happy to let the relationship progress in its own way.

Later, when we had been dating for a few weeks, we decided that we wanted to take our relationship to a more physical level. By this time, I had already moved into her house. At first it was more of a business arrangement. She had a three-bedroom house and I was living in a hotel. We tried to fool ourselves into thinking that it was a platonic living arrangement, but we both knew where we would soon end up.

Those first few weeks with Marcia were magical. Whenever I needed to talk about something – even something that might have seemed trivial to others – she was always there to listen. Slowly, I was opening up to her, letting her in to my nightmares from work. I still thought that I would be able to solve the problems on my own.

It was also great having the privacy that a house provided. I no longer heard guests in adjoining rooms. There was a nice little yard with a dog running around. Marcia even encouraged me to grill food for us on the back porch, and I wowed her with my slow-cooked barbecued ribs. I was finally beginning to feel more at home in Birmingham.

We were both caught up in the moment one night, drinking

each other in with our eyes. As we made our way into the bedroom, all I could think about was making love to the woman who was helping me get through the toughest time I had ever faced. But it wouldn't happen that night. Because of my anxiety, something happened to me that had never happened before; I was impotent.

It wasn't an isolated incident, either. Marcia and I were both frustrated by my physical condition. She was afraid that I wasn't attracted to her. It hurt her pride and mine. At first, Marcia became angry. I couldn't blame her, because I was angry, too. Eventually, though, we worked through our feelings and talked it out. We began to see that my work-related anxiety was having more of an effect on me than I wanted to admit.

5

PARADISE LOST

If we see a light at the end of a tunnel,
It's the light of an oncoming train.
–Robert Lowell, "Day by Day"

Birmingham, Alabama
December 1993

I ran for my life through the fog, tripping over railroad ties
and wooden beams. Hornbuckle and Thomasson were hot
on my trail. I could hear their sadistic laughter behind me. I
had no sense of direction and sought only to get as far from
the diesel shop as I could. The harder I ran, the longer the
yard seemed. I was going nowhere. Sweat poured from my
face, and my hands bled from falls to the graveled ground.

Finally, I found what looked like a safe place to hide. I entered the old shack and nearly ripped the rotten door off its
hinges. I chose a corner and squatted down. My breath came
in gasps. There were no sounds of my pursuers. Suddenly, I
looked up and they were right in front of me. Hornbuckle had
a piece of pipe in his hands and Thomasson twirled a length
rope. They walked slowly towards me. There was no escape. I
screamed – and woke up.

Nightmares became a frequent part of my nightly routine.
It took me a couple hours of tossing and turning before I could
finally fall asleep. Then, after only three or four hours, I would
bolt awake in bed. My nightclothes were soaked with sweat

and I was disoriented. Marcia usually woke with me if it was an off day and I was in bed before the sun rose. Immediately upon waking, I started to dread going into work.

I needed the full day to psych myself up to get ready for work. Up at around noon, I spent the next nine or so hours making excuses to myself about why I wouldn't be able to go in. I fought a mental battle. I wanted to call in sick. I wanted to leave town. I wanted anything to get out of having to face Hornbuckle and Thomasson.

The joy I normally found in servicing trains was fading fast. It used to be a thrill when a giant locomotive rolled into the shop for repairs and servicing. I imagined men like Grandfather Martin and my dad engineering the trains from points across the country. I thought of my job as important and exciting. Slowly, Hornbuckle and Thomasson were destroying the image.

I *had* to enter the office to retrieve the printouts. There was no other way around it. Whenever I entered the office, though, Hornbuckle would subject me to crude words and physical attacks. He was as regular as a train schedule. It was a no-win situation. Unfortunately, I couldn't see that.

For a while, I decided that I could – and must – deal with whatever was thrown at me. I felt like I'd gotten my second wind. I entered the office with newfound strength and refused to let Hornbuckle and Thomasson get to me. Besides physically pushing them out of the way, I yelled at them to stop. I talked of nothing but railroad business. I felt like I was making strides, but Hornbuckle and Thomasson were like overzealous nine-year-olds. They didn't know when to quit – and didn't feel they had to. My hopes of ignoring them dissolved.

As bad as it was when I first arrived in Birmingham, the physical and verbal assaults got worse. The pinches on my rear were humiliating and painful, but if that would be the extent of things, I still thought I could cope with the situation. Hornbuckle and Thomasson proved me wrong once again as they ganged up on me.

Thomasson was the first to take things further. Early one morning, around four o'clock, while Hornbuckle sat behind the desk shuffling through paperwork, Thomasson came in behind me. I was reviewing some of the printouts and wasn't paying attention to anything around me.

Suddenly, I felt an arm grab me around the neck. More quickly than I could respond, Thomasson had me in a headlock. I struggled to get loose. He slowly bent me over the desk and began moving his hands over me. Hornbuckle watched the entire struggle. I felt my face flush with anger and humiliation as Thomasson's hands traveled over my buttocks. He thrust his hands between my legs and up towards my genitals.

I finally gathered the strength to break loose from the headlock and kicked away. I turned around to a grinning Hornbuckle and Thomasson. I felt crazed, on the brink between sanity and violence. *This is crazy,* I thought. *I'm going to kill somebody – or something's got to give.* I felt helpless against them. My mind reeled as I tried to think of a way to make them stop without putting myself at risk of retaliation or getting fired. Nothing came to mind.

For the rest of my shift, I stayed away from the office. I spent the time finishing up the trains that were already in the service center. It was a long night and my nerves were shattered. Finally, I watched the sun come up and knew it would be time to go home shortly. I needed to hold on to Marcia and hear her tell me that everything was going to be all right.

Marcia did not tell me that all was well, though. Instead, she was horrified as I told her what happened to me.

"Eddie, you've got to tell someone about this. Hornbuckle's boss has got to know. This thing is killing you," she told me.

I was stubborn and still thought that I could get things straightened out on my own. I was brought up in a very male-dominated environment where I was taught to fight when necessary. In high school I had been in a few fights. I wasn't a real tough guy, but I could take care of myself. For me to give in to Hornbuckle and Thomasson would have been a personal failure. I don't like to fail and I don't like to lose. I tried to handle the irrational men with the one thing they couldn't seem to grasp: reason.

The next evening at work, I confronted Hornbuckle for what felt like the tenth time. I entered the office and walked up to his desk. He looked up at me with his usual sneer.

"Look, something's got to be done," I told him. "I can't do my job with you guys messing with me like this. Thomasson won't listen to a word I say. You and he have got to leave me the hell alone. My work is suffering. I don't want someone killed because I'm not concentrating on my job."

If I expected anything from Hornbuckle, I was disappointed. He merely sat at his desk and regarded me with a smirk across his face. I waited a few moments before turning on my heels and walking out. I reassured myself that even if he hadn't said anything, he now knew how badly things were getting out of hand. He had to respond to my complaint.

Later that night, I entered the office to retrieve some paperwork. When I squeezed by the desk, again I felt Hornbuckle's hand pinch my rear.

"Damn it!" I yelled. "I asked you guys to stop this!"

"You've got a cute ass," said a grinning Hornbuckle. "I'd like to bend you over this desk and fuck you in the ass."

I left in a daze. I was completely baffled and couldn't believe his nerve. People just didn't act like this. Railroad men were supposed to be my brothers, but here I had a gang of men who seemed to be acting like enemies. I was confused. Hornbuckle had a wife at home. Neither he nor Thomasson seemed homosexual, and yet they kept talking to me in a sexual manner and constantly touched, groped, and fondled me. I felt like I was in prison with two sexually deviant men who were determined to overpower me.

Things deteriorated more during the next few weeks. I wasn't sleeping. I wasn't eating and lost a lot of weight. My work was not impressive, and I wasn't concentrating on all of the tasks I was responsible for. Instead, I was wishing that I had eyes in the back of my head. I thought of the uncomplicated life I had led in Greenville. It seemed like years ago and thousands of miles away.

Even a short trip to Greenville to visit my family during Christmas didn't help me feel any better. I missed my children terribly. I missed the house I had been building by hand for the past few years. I thought of simple pleasures like weekend golf games with old buddies. I was far from home.

In the weeks ahead, Hornbuckle and Thomasson stepped up their assaults and dangerous games. They must have sensed my fears. They were like animals that smelled blood. Every time I turned around, it seemed that one of them was behind me. They began to play malicious tricks on me like hiding my keys.

I had keys to lock and unlock one of the most important safety controls – the derailer. If a locomotive runs over it, it derails the train on purpose to protect us while we work. I had to have the keys with me at all times. A couple of times, I laid them on the desk in the office. When I turned around, they had disappeared. I couldn't operate the derailers without the keys. The Federal Railroad Administration charged huge fines for companies violating the safety procedures. Also, Norfolk Southern could fire me for violating any safety system.

"Come on, guys! Where the heck are my keys?" I yelled.

Hornbuckle and Thomasson answered me with shrugged shoulders and giggles. I thought of the saying, "It's all fun and games until somebody puts an eye out." Losing an eye on the railroad was the least of your worries if a safety system wasn't in place. It was losing a life that I was worried about.

As a further reminder of just how important my keys were, I thought about the key my mother had given to me for my chain. It had once belonged to her cousin who was also a railroad man. He had died years earlier, before I was born. The key was cut perfectly in half by the wheels of a train – as it lay in my mother's cousin's pocket. So, I drilled a hole in it and put it on my key chain. That key had been with me from my first day of work on the railroad. It was a sobering reminder that accidents can happen.

I stormed out of the office and did what work I could on the trains that were still in the service area. Sooner or later, though, I knew they'd have to be moved. I needed my keys. I walked back in the office and there, sitting exactly where I had first laid them down, were my keys. I retrieved them wordlessly and left the office. I heard Hornbuckle and Thomasson laughing as I shut the door behind me.

For some sick reason, Hornbuckle loved telling me that I was "pretty." I sat in the office reading over some paperwork. Hornbuckle was changing the printer paper. As he took off the bundle of perforated paper, he fashioned it over my head to look like a scarf. With the top of his hand, he held on to the top of my head while bunching the paper under my chin with his other. Before I could knock his hands and the paper away, he said, "Ooh, doesn't Eddie look so pretty?" Over in the corner, Thomasson blew me a kiss.

Hornbuckle and Thomasson didn't direct their rude comments only to me. I often heard them use racial slurs when describing some of the black men who worked in the yard. They described Cheatham, the man who had helped train me, as a "lazy nigger." For a while, there was a female service attendant working at the Norris yard. Hornbuckle was fond of telling everyone that she "had to move her balls out of the way before getting fucked." They had "colorful" comments for just about everyone.

They often talked about Marcia. Shortly before some requested time off, Hornbuckle asked me if I was "taking my cunt with me for the weekend." That was a favorite word of his and he used it often. If Marcia called the office to speak with me, he often said, "Eddie, it's your cunt calling for you." When I got off work, he asked if my "cunt" was waiting for me at home. As much as I was bothered by their abuse of me, I was even angrier that they'd refer to Marcia using such language. They only laughed when I asked them to stop.

Thomasson was more of a physical assailant than Horn-buckle. He enjoyed intimidating me with sudden motions to-ward me or by blowing kisses at me. On one occasion, during a shift change, he came up behind me like he was going to get me in a headlock. Because he had done it before, I was ready for him. We scuffled across the room. I was knocked into Hornbuckle's locker (which was never locked). Some of the contents in the locker spilled out. A handful of other men wit-nessed the incident and chalked it up to Thomasson and me horsing around. They found the entire incident amusing and had no idea why I was so angry.

I left all of the paperwork behind that morning. I left the yard. I don't know how I made it home. My vision was clouded with rage and humiliation. My hands shook as I gripped the steering wheel tightly.

❖   ❖

Red Summerlin was never part of the normal routine. The only times I saw him were during shift changes. He worked the second shift in the same capacity that I did, as a mechani-cal supervisor. He was a strange bird. He observed a lot of the abuse directed towards me. Often, at the beginning of my shift, he sat in the office talking with Hornbuckle. He was as much a fixture there as the desk.

Hornbuckle came in early for work and used the place as a hangout. It was his version of a bar. Hornbuckle and Summerlin's lives revolved completely around the railroad. They often talked for an hour or so between shifts. As they sat next to the window facing the service area, they commented on the servicemen who walked by.

As someone passed, Hornbuckle said things like, "There goes that gay son-of-a-bitch. He isn't worth a flying fuck. His mother must have done an Aborigine." Hornbuckle wasn't a clever man and often didn't sound like he knew what he was talking about. It was like he tried to come up with as much vulgarity as possible in one insult.

Another typical Hornbuckle observation was, "I bet that guy could suck a good dick. I bet he's got a eency-weency penis. His wife's probably fucking two or three guys while he's at work. He probably has more sex with his dog than he does with his wife." After each comment, Hornbuckle and Summerlin would laugh hysterically.

I was talking to Marcia on the phone at about 10:30 one night. Hornbuckle and Summerlin were talking in the background. I swiveled my chair around so that I didn't have to observe them. It was fine with me if they wanted to talk about other servicemen – anything for them to stop messing with me. Marcia and I talked about plans for the upcoming weekend. I wasn't paying much attention to the men behind me, but I instinctively turned when I heard my name mentioned.

As I turned, Hornbuckle said to Summerlin, "Well, hell. Show Eddie your tattoo."

There were rumors going around the yard about Summerlin's tattoo. I heard all sorts of things about what the former Navy SEAL had painted on his rear. The rumors ranged from the bizarre to the downright gross. Before I knew what he was doing, Summerlin stood up and turned his back to me. Marcia was still talking into the phone.

In one motion, Summerlin dropped his pants and underwear. He bent over. As offensive as it was for Summerlin's rear end and genitals to be hanging in my view, the tattoo was worse. There, covering one side of his rear, was a picture of a large rooster. The rooster's head was bent down towards Summerlin's anus. In its beak was a worm. The worm was drawn to look like it was coming from inside his anus. I turned away in disgust.

"Oh, my God," I breathed into the phone.

"What? What is it?" asked Marcia, alarmed.

"You're not gonna' believe this. Summerlin just showed me his tattoo," I told her.

"What was it?" she asked. I described it briefly.

"That is the grossest thing I have ever heard," she said. "What the heck's wrong with him? You need to get out of there." I sensed the urgency and worry in her voice. How could she not be worried? I couldn't think of anyone having to be exposed to something like that at work. To Marcia, a dental hygienist, it was unthinkable to have a co-worker bend over and expose a tattoo that centered around the anus. After having seen the tattoo, I couldn't get the picture out of my mind. It was crazy.

Summerlin, from that moment on, seemed to participate more and more in the verbal vulgarities. He, too, took to referring to Marcia as my "cunt." Another favorite expression of his was, "All right, boys, this is a pecker check. Get 'em out." Summerlin also greeted me in the way Hornbuckle had with "Can I see your dick?"

At the end of one particularly busy shift, I entered the office to complete the final paperwork. I wasn't paying attention to Hornbuckle and Thomasson. They seemed busy with paperwork of their own. Suddenly, I felt an arm around my neck. Again, Thomasson bent me over the desk. This time, though, Hornbuckle was not merely a spectator.

Hornbuckle picked up a broom and walked slowly over to where I was struggling. I couldn't seem to throw Thomasson off of my body. His face was close to mine and I could feel his hot, foul breath on my neck. I froze with fear. This can not be happening to me. Hornbuckle approached me and told me that I had a "real cute ass" and that I was "very pretty." He turned the broomstick around and held the handle towards my rear end.

He traveled the length of my leg with the end of the broomstick. It crept closer and closer to my rear end. Then, he pushed the handle around my anus and cackled at my discomfort. He tried to force it into my anus. My blood felt like it was boiling, and my vision was fading fast from the anger. Finally, I kicked my leg back and fought them off. They laughed maniacally.

"Stop this crap right now!" I croaked. My voice was raw with rage.

"Look," Hornbuckle said, "You're just going to have to learn to get along with the boys. If that means letting them play with your dick and balls, then that's what you gotta do."

"I can tell you right now that that's not going to happen," I responded. I slowly backed away from them.

"Then I'll run your sweet ass off the property."

On another occasion, I was reading a pink copy of a form put in my box regarding my medical coverage. Hornbuckle was shooting the breeze with Thomasson, sitting in their usual place by the window. As always, whatever I was doing seemed to capture their attention.

"Hey, what is that, Eddie?" asked Hornbuckle.

I ignored him and continued reading.

"It looks like mortgage papers."

Again, I tried to ignore him.

"Listen," he said, "I wouldn't bother getting a house here. You're not going to be here that long."

6

BRICK WALLS

Eddie, this is absolutely ridiculous," said Marcia angrily. "These men are tearing you apart." She sat down beside me on the couch and put her arm on my shoulder.

"I know, I know. But what the heck can I do about it? I can't lose this job," I told her. I rubbed my temples with my hands. It seemed that for the past couple months I had a constant headache.

"Go see Hornbuckle's boss – what's-his-name?" she said.

"Benson. Gerald Benson. I tried going to him twice in December, but he didn't do anything then. I'm stuck here."

Marcia shook her head in disbelief.

Benson had done nothing for me when I first told him about the crude remarks made to me by Hornbuckle and Thomasson. Marcia was adamant about my seeing him. She was right, too. I thought that maybe now, with all of the other horrible things they had done to me, Benson might take my complaints seriously. I told Marcia that I would go see Benson the next morning. She seemed relieved.

I was far from being relieved. I knew from experience that while the wheels on a locomotive turned quickly, that wasn't

53

always the case when you needed upper management to act on something. I remembered going to Benson the first week of December. It was after Hornbuckle pinched me on the rear and asked to see my penis. The first-shift general foreman laughed as I told him the story.

"You're just going to have to get along with those guys," were Benson's words of wisdom. He didn't seem to care in the least.

"Well, I can't handle it," I'd told him.

Benson shrugged his shoulders and went back to reading. The meeting was over.

The second time I talked with Benson in December, I felt a little better. I was more forceful in my protests to him. I told him that Hornbuckle and Thomasson were distracting me from my job. It was hard for me to learn a new position with so many distractions. Benson seemed more concerned as I talked to him, no doubt because railroad work was being upset. He had me go into detail on a few of the incidents. I walked out of the office thinking that he might finally put a stop to the assaults. I was wrong, again.

After I talked to Benson the second time, Hornbuckle and Thomasson were worse than ever. I might as well have complained to a brick wall, for all the good it did me. They say that the third time's the charm, and Marcia seemed to be banking on that being true. I hoped it was. I didn't want that kind of humiliation again.

Hornbuckle and Thomasson had moved far beyond asking to see my "dick." This time, Benson couldn't possibly think it was funny. A reasonable man could see that these were no acts of "horseplay." These were out-and-out physical attacks. Benson was my only chance of getting these men to leave me alone.

It was extremely embarrassing for me to tell anyone, let alone another man, about what was happening to me at work. I knew that Marcia would never judge me, but others weren't so kind. I imagined Benson snickering about it after I left the office. I imagined the servicemen I supervised gossiping about Hornbuckle and Thomasson's treatment of me.

I knew that everyone thought it was my fault, that I had somehow brought these things upon myself. In short, I had become completely paranoid.

I tried to reassure myself that I had gone through the proper channels so far. From my first day on the job, I had been taught to always follow the chain of command. I knew that with any problem, you first went to your immediate supervisor. He was supposed to look into the matter and try to help you rectify the problem. I had a unique case, though – my problem concerned my immediate supervisor.

I felt that when I talked to Hornbuckle about his treatment of me, I was attempting to do the impossible. Hornbuckle was impervious to my pleas. He was a man who felt wholly secure in his position. And why shouldn't he? After all, Hornbuckle's boss had taken no action against him when I complained. He was sitting high and in no danger of losing his job. He was on tight terms with all the men at Birmingham. I was the outsider.

There was another reason I was concerned about seeking Benson's help: he had personally witnessed several harassment incidents and had done nothing to stop them. Because Benson was the first-shift general foreman, his first hour in the morning overlapped my (third shift's) last hour. He was sometimes in the office when Hornbuckle called Marcia "a cunt" or talked about my "cute ass." Not once did he ever tell Hornbuckle that he was acting improperly. On the contrary, he seemed to find it amusing.

The next morning, at around 7:30, I waited until Hornbuckle and Thomasson left for home. Then, I entered the office to talk with Benson. He wore dress slacks and a button-down oxford, both completely free of any grease. Again I thought, *this guy is just counting his days to retirement.* He doesn't want to rock the boat.

"Mr. Benson, something's got to give with Hornbuckle," I told him nervously. I sat down in front of his desk.

"What do you mean?" he asked.

It was extremely difficult for me to tell him about the physical assaults, but I knew that if I wanted Hornbuckle and Thomasson to stop, I had to.

"Sir, I talked to you about Hornbuckle and Thomasson a couple times last month. They just won't leave me alone. Now, they've started–" I was too embarrassed to go on.

"Started what?" he asked, half listening to me. He was reading through the daily paperwork and trying to organize his day. He might have been thinking about where he would be going to lunch later. He was doing anything but giving me his complete attention.

I gathered the strength to go on. I told him about being manhandled by both men on numerous occasions. I told him about the crude talk and insults. Benson laughed when I told him how Thomasson had put me in headlocks and tried to fondle my genitals.

I talked to him for a full five minutes about what I'd been subjected to. Every once in a while, he nodded or mumbled a "go on." I never got his full attention.

When I finally finished telling him what was done to me, he looked up. He stared at me for a few moments as if trying to read me. I began feeling paranoid. Benson was known around the yard as a man of few words, so I didn't expect much of a reply from him. He had a small smile when he spoke.

"Well, okay. All right," he told me.

I figured that meant he had heard everything and would act upon the information I'd given him. Besides, what had been done to me couldn't fall into any gray area between right and wrong. It didn't take much sense to determine the severity of the situation. I could have told him one story of Thomasson's assault and that would have been enough.

I wanted to hear something more from Benson before I left.

"So?" I asked him.

Benson regarded me coolly for a moment. His face turned into a smirk and he gave me a small chuckle. "They're just fucking with you, Eddie," he told me.

"Well, I can't handle it," I told him. "I've already tried. That's why I came to you."

Benson nodded his head in understanding, and went back to his paperwork. I finally went home. I had done what I needed to do. I fully expected results, especially after the horrible things I'd reported. A supervisor couldn't ignore things anymore. It had gone too far.

Over the next few days, absolutely nothing happened. They were not asked to report to Benson. There were no letters of reprimand in their boxes. Nothing came of my conversation with Benson at all. Hornbuckle and Thomasson continued with their assaults. It seemed that all was lost.

I came to grips that I was dealing with the "good old boy's" network. It was evident in businesses across the country, but it was most widespread where unions existed. The railroad was union-run and union strong. My promotion had called for me to give up my union membership. I was considered management. However, Hornbuckle and Benson still held on to their union ties.

There was also the fact that I was an outsider. It didn't matter that I was a Southerner, born and raised. It didn't matter that I was a dyed-in-the-wool railroad man. All that mattered was that I had moved to Birmingham and taken over a job that everyone thought their buddy would get. I was not from the Alabama railroad as most of the men were.

For Benson to act on my complaints meant that he'd have to go against his union comrade, Hornbuckle. The same went for Thomasson. The three men had known each other for many years and over many beers. They buckled together to face what they perceived as the "outside threat": me. I was left without a leg to stand on.

I didn't subscribe to turning a blind eye on something wrong to protect a fellow union member. I was raised to be honest. Once, in Spartanburg, South Carolina, I turned in my supervisor to railroad authorities for theft and misuse of company property. He had taken a company truck that we all were supposed to have access to, and began using it as his personal vehicle. Also, he stole metal material, tools, plywood, and janitorial supplies from the company. I couldn't stand him abusing his power, so I called the internal auditor and turned him in. My whistle-blowing contributed to a bad working relationship with the man, especially when he was only reprimanded for his actions. However, I knew that I had done the right thing. I didn't understand how Benson and Hornbuckle could act the way they did.

Marcia was shocked when Benson didn't help me. She couldn't believe that he could sit on his rear and ignore the problems.

I became completely withdrawn and didn't want to set foot out of the house. I didn't sleep or eat. I spent most of my time staring at a television screen. I didn't care what was on. Marcia turned off the television and sat down beside me. She had to call my name a couple times before I even noticed the television was off. She asked about Benson's boss and whether or not I could go to him.

Master mechanic Tom Bennett oversaw the Birmingham facility and several others in the region. I knew that when it came to reporting Hornbuckle and Thomasson, Bennett was not an option. In the two months I was at the facility, I hadn't once seen Bennett in the yard. As the man who's in charge of making sure the yard is run correctly, it seemed to me that he should be there in person every once in a while. I never trusted bosses who didn't know what went on under their noses. A couple of times before, on unrelated incidents, I had needed to get in touch with Bennett. It was nearly impossible. He was never in his office or available by phone.

I saw more of the same happening if I went to Bennett. There was a rumor that he was about to retire. I imagined he'd treat the situation with the same disinterest that Benson had. I didn't want to keep telling the stories, either. I hated to talk about how Hornbuckle and Thomasson took advantage of me that way. It hurt my pride discussing it. If things didn't work out with Bennett, I'd have to go to his boss, then to his boss, and so on. I began to see the future as futile.

I always saw myself working for the railroad until I retired. I was still a relatively young man of thirty-nine. I had worked for the railroad for fourteen years and had many more left in me. I was making about $40,000 a year as a mechanical supervisor and had all of the benefits, including a 401(k) retirement savings plan. Eventually, if I did my job well, I could rise as high as general foreman. I couldn't see life getting any sweeter, especially since I had no college degree. This was supposed to be the gravy boat, but it was leaking fast.

I spent many sleepless hours after one shift thinking about my future. I was completely turned around from where I wanted to be. Hornbuckle and Thomasson were taking my life from me, and I was letting them do it. The future seemed pointless. Irrational thoughts crept into my head, things I had never thought about before. I thought about ending the charade once and for all with firepower.

I owned several guns. It would be so easy to wait until I was alone in the house and fix the problem. I could load a pistol or a shotgun. I'd have to make sure that no one else was around outside. Then, with a simple squeeze of the trigger, the barrel pointed just right, my problems would be over.

I tried to shake those thoughts from my mind. They scared me. I used to love life with all of its ups and downs. Now, there was nothing but downs. Marcia and my children were the only people keeping me from doing something stupid. She wanted me to fight, but I felt like there was no fight left in me.

My panic attacks increased. It felt like I had a big secret and I was scared it was going to show. I feared that people knew what was happening to me and thought that I was the problem. I was completely transparent, and people were able to see through me and know what I was thinking. I was ashamed of what Hornbuckle and Thomasson were putting me through. It consumed me.

Marcia talked to me about the problems she had gone through with her abusive husband. At the time, she said, she never thought the nightmare would end. Eventually, though, it did. She believed that things happened for a reason. Maybe, she mused, it was time for me to move on from the railroad.

At first, I dismissed any thoughts of getting out of railroad work. It was all I cared about. Slowly, though, it dawned on me that I hadn't cared about the railroad since moving to Birmingham. How could I anymore? The railroad had betrayed me.

Marcia was a fighter. She had fought her way out of a bad marriage and found a way back to a normal life. She was not going to let me give up on myself. She told me that she had been in a sick place for a long time, without any choices. I still had choices. She helped me to see that. No matter what it took, I had to get away from the stranglehold the railroad had on my life.

On those rare occasions when sleep found me, Marcia often stayed awake and watched me doze. She said that I never looked more at peace than when I slept. Whatever nightmares were raging in my head, my face looked happy. Marcia was determined to help me get through the nightmares. She made me talk about them when I woke up. She didn't want me bottling up anything anymore. It was dangerous to keep the fear to myself.

No one in my family knew about my problems. Unlike Marcia's family – loud and crazy, but the type that tells you what's going on – my family didn't discuss much of anything. I couldn't go to my parents with problems of any kind. As a child, I was taught to sit down and shut up. We didn't discuss things like feelings or problems. The only one I felt I might be able to talk to was my sister, Lynn.

I hadn't yet talked to Lynn about anything that was going on at work. Lynn managed the rental properties I owned in Greenville, and I often talked with her about business. I felt that she might have a good perspective about what to do in my current situation. She always had good advice for me when I needed it.

Lynn was a graduate of the University of Georgia in Athens. She is five years older than I am, so we barely knew each other when we were growing up. She always had her own friends and plans. She was off to college before I even entered high school. I never hung around her as a child.

As we grew older, Lynn and I developed a closer relationship. She was a level-headed mother of two and seemed to always have good advice when it came to fixing problems. She was the only one I felt safe leaving in charge of my rentals and dogs. She also took over the project of building the home I had worked on for the past few years.

I finally called her one evening when I was feeling desperate. I tried to talk about things that didn't matter. I was embarrassed to talk to my sister about being sexually assaulted. After all, I was a man and should have been able to take care of myself. That's what my father would have told me. I never felt so helpless and weak in all of my life. Lynn immediately sensed that something was wrong.

After some persuasion, I let it all out. It felt great to talk about it with someone from my family. I told her about the crude comments. I told her about the pinching of my rear. I told her about the headlocks. I told her about the broom handle incident. I had tears of rage and shame falling from my eyes, but I went on. I explained to Lynn about going to Benson on three occasions and nothing being done. She listened to it all.

Then, she told me what I needed to do. Before, I had never considered seeking the kind of help she suggested. It seemed like I would be blowing things out of proportion. But the more I thought about it, the better it sounded. It was time to fight back in the only way I could.

"Eddie," said Lynn, "You need to get yourself an attorney."

7

A SHADOW OF A MAN

I knew you'd break me down and leave me flat
I saw it coming but I turned my back
I feel like a nickel on the railroad track
–David Allen, "Blue Train"

Birmingham, Alabama
March 1994

The life I had once known and loved was gone. Every day was a new journey into fear, a living nightmare that I couldn't wake from. Because I decided to confront my attackers through an attorney, I knew that my time in the locomotive industry would soon be over. Once I left Norfolk Southern, that would be the end of my family's history and involvement with the railroad.

I contacted an attorney the day after talking to my sister in January. I opened up the Birmingham yellow pages and literally let my fingers do the walking. I settled on the name of Beverly P. Baker. I don't know what made me stop my finger on her name. I didn't have any idea about what type of law she specialized in. I didn't know what type of experience she had. I didn't know what type of person she was. It was a lucky decision.

I called Ms. Baker and told her a little about what was going on with me. She was a good listener. She told me that she might be able to help me. We set an appointment for a week later. It was an extremely big step for me to take, and I began having doubts about talking to an attorney. It seemed too extreme. I felt like I was making a big deal out of a little thing that I should have handled myself. It didn't matter that I could barely function anymore. It didn't matter that Hornbuckle and Thomasson were making life a living hell for me. I still thought that I could fix things on my own. I didn't show up for our appointment.

About a month later, I changed my mind. Things at work were still horrible. I was mentally exhausted and physically sick. One day, I opened my locker to discover a dead fish wrapped in a newspaper. I calmly took it out to the parking lot garbage can and deposited it. I later found out that this was a death threat, made popular in the Godfather movies. I called Beverly Baker again and made another appointment. I went down to the Haskell Slaughter Young & Johnston office in downtown Birmingham to meet with her.

As I walked in to the nicely decorated offices, the receptionist greeted me. After I told her who I was and who I had an appointment with, she told me to have a seat. I was kept waiting for only a minute before Beverly came out. She was an attractive, middle-aged black woman with kind eyes. We introduced ourselves to each other and went into a conference room. We sat down at the huge table and she offered me some refreshments.

Beverly asked me to tell her everything, from how I first started work in Birmingham to the problems with my co-workers. I took her through a brief history of my work with the railroad. Then, hesitantly, I led her through the nightmare of working at the Norris diesel shop. It was difficult to tell the horrible things to a complete stranger, but she made it easy. She listened thoughtfully to all that I told her, stopping me only when she needed something explained.

I finished and waited for her judgment. I was afraid that she would tell me this was not a problem for a lawyer and that I should talk to railroad personnel. My stomach was churning. She looked at me with her dark eyes and told me the one thing I had needed to hear from an authority figure: I was being wronged. Beverly told me that I possibly had a case of sexual harassment. Then, she asked me if I wanted her help to fix the problems.

Gratefully, I accepted her offer. I told her that she was my last line of defense. We shook hands and I immediately felt better. It was the help that I needed to beat my harassers. I finally felt like I had a chance of winning. We made an appointment for the next day so that I could sign the necessary paperwork.

Our agreement was standard. The firm of Haskell Slaughter Young & Johnston would take the case on straight contingency. If the case was settled before we went to court or before any action was taken, the firm received twenty percent of the settlement. If the case went through the complete legal process and we settled at the courthouse door, the fee was raised to thirty percent. If we went to trial and there was a jury verdict, they got forty percent.

It didn't matter to me how much the firm took home. It didn't matter to me if I ever saw a penny. I just wanted something to stop the horrors at work. Now, I had the law on my side. And from the looks of the offices, it was a very successful law firm.

We brought formal charges against Norfolk Southern Corporation, Larry Hornbuckle, Preston Thomasson, and Robert Summerlin. Citing the Federal Employers' Liability Act (FELA), the Equal Employment Opportunity Commission (EEOC), and various state laws, the defendants were charged. Included were charges of sexual harassment under Title VII of the Civil Rights Act of 1964, outrage (an Alabama claim having to do with distress beyond all possible bounds of decency), intentional infliction of emotional distress, invasion of privacy, negligence, and assault and battery.

I had no idea that there were so many laws dealing with the

behavior I was subjected to. After discussing the many charges with Beverly, I was sure that I had made the right decision.

To sue any railroad operating in the United States, the plain-tiff must bring any charges under FELA. Since the federal government regulates railroads, this type of lawsuit may not be brought under any other statute. The FELA mandated that it was the railroad's obligation to furnish a reasonably safe workplace for its employees. Also, the railroad was responsible for providing proper supervision, help for employees, and the enforcement of safety and departmental rules. As Beverly explained the FELA to me, I knew that the railroad had failed me on these obligations.

In order to file a lawsuit against Norfolk Southern, I also needed permission from the EEOC. Beverly had me fill out a standard complaint form to be sent to the commission. In it, I wrote down both what had been done to me and why I felt that I'd been sexually harassed.

I knew that I could never turn back after I filed with the EEOC. I sucked in my breath and handed the form over to Beverly. She assured me that everything would be all right.

After I'd filled out the proper paperwork and signed my name to numerous affidavits, Beverly suggested I go see a doctor of my choice. She was worried about my long list of alarming physical and psychological symptoms. I grudgingly agreed. I hated to see doctors. They made me uncomfortable. However, I knew that it was necessary and overdue. I hadn't felt well in a long time.

I updated Marcia on the lawsuit. She reaffirmed that I was doing the right thing. She seemed happy that I was finally standing up and doing something about my situation. She gave me the name of a doctor that she'd seen a couple times. She told me that he was a good physician and genuinely cared about his patients. I made an appointment.

Dr. Curtis Toliver was a general practitioner. I walked into his Gardendale office in the early afternoon. While waiting for my appointment, I filled out the necessary insurance forms in the waiting room. I wondered if there was a miracle drug that could accommodate all of my symptoms. I didn't wait long and was soon called into an examining room.

I was extremely nervous as I walked back the hallway. I began having a mild panic attack. There was something about the sterile environment, the disease and sickness that passed through the doors every hour, and the possibility of Dr. Toliver telling me that I was extremely sick. My hands shook, my face was flushed, and I was scared. My voice rattled when I tried to speak.

There was something calming about Dr. Toliver and I quickly relaxed. I was sitting on the paper-covered examining table when he walked into the room. He was an older man with gray hair and a kind face. He had a blank file folder in his hands that contained only my weight and height. He sensed that something was wrong with me immediately. He took one look at my six-foot two-inch frame and knew that I was not a patient complaining of a cold.

I must have looked horrible. There I was, shaking and nervous. My skin was pasty white except for my face, which was flushed red. I was a walking skeleton. My clothes literally hung off of me.

When I began work in Birmingham, I weighed a healthy 205 pounds. That was my weight, give or take a couple pounds, for the last twenty years of my life. After the problems at work began and I lost my appetite and my weight quickly dropped. When I sat down in Dr. Toliver's examining room, I weighed only 168 pounds. Dr. Toliver wanted to know what had made me lose over 35 pounds.

He was easy to talk to. I went through my story in great detail. He was horrified at what I told him. I told him about the symptoms I had and how I felt most of the time. Dr. Toliver shook his head in disbelief. He told me, "That's the most terrible thing I've ever heard." I was relieved that a doctor believed in me.

He seemed to take a personal stake in my problems, commenting about what Hornbuckle and company deserved. He was very direct. Dr. Toliver knew what he would have done: he mentioned "knocking the hell out of somebody." He didn't understand how I took it for so long. I told him that had I done anything physical, I could have lost my job. That made him even angrier.

After checking all of my vital signs and asking about my symptoms in detail, Dr. Toliver left the room for a moment. When he returned, he held a syringe filled with a clear liquid. He swabbed my arm with alcohol and explained that he was giving me a sedative. He suggested that I seek some counseling services and get away from work for a while. He also told me that he wanted me to go home immediately and get some sleep. That sounded like a good idea to me, but I doubted that I'd be able to. After all, I hadn't slept in months.

I thanked Dr. Toliver for his time and settled my bill and the insurance forms. I drove the short distance home and sat down on the bed. Half an hour later, I was in a deep, uninterrupted sleep. I hadn't slept very well since I left South Carolina, but the sedative knocked me out for a couple of days.

During this time, my attorney and I were waiting to get the charge back from the EEOC that said we could go ahead and sue Norfolk Southern. It arrived, and Beverly officially filed the lawsuit. They would send a copy to Norfolk Southern and file a copy with the courthouse.

I assumed, incorrectly, that the rest of the lawsuit would be uneventful. I knew that Hornbuckle, Thomasson, and Summerlin would eventually find out that they were being charged in a lawsuit. I figured I'd cross that bridge when I came to it.

On April 4, 1994, ten days after we filed with the EEOC, Norfolk Southern got their copy of the lawsuit. At around eleven o'clock that night, I was flagged down in the diesel shop parking lot by my subordinate, Curtis Brierly. I rolled the window down and he came up to my truck. He didn't greet me in the traditional way.

"What's going on?" he asked me. I could hear the concern in his voice.

"What do you mean?" I asked back.

He said, "Well I heard today that you filed a sexual harassment suit against Hornbuckle."

The hairs on the back of my neck stood on end. Alarmed, I asked Brierly where he'd heard this. It was not supposed to be public knowledge. My emotions were mixed. On the one hand, I was embarrassed that my co-workers knew all about my personal business; on the other, I was angry that Norfolk Southern had allowed word to leak out.

"Well, everybody on the yard knows about it," he said.

Oh my God, I thought. *I'm getting ready to walk into a crossfire here – guns are gonna be blazing.* Brierly told me that I had really opened a can of worms and that I had better be careful.

Hesitantly, I parked the truck and took a long look around. Railroad men do not like it when one of their own goes to outside help to solve a railroad problem. I had not only gone to outside help, I might as well have been to Timbuktu. *Everybody in the yard knows,* Brierly had told me. That meant that everybody knew about the trouble I'd been having. That meant having to deal with glares from co-workers who thought I couldn't solve my own problems.

I went onto the yard for my shift. Apparently, everybody knew about the lawsuit except Hornbuckle. He hadn't been there the whole day. Foolishly I thought – but only for an instant – that maybe Hornbuckle wouldn't find out about it that night. I was surprised that nobody had called him and told him the news.

When Hornbuckle came to work, I sucked in my breath. He gave me the usual rude greeting when he saw me in the office and sat down at his desk. He shuffled through the night's paperwork.

He was staring at the computer when his phone rang. He greeted the caller and looked like he was about to launch into a conversation when his facial expression changed. I could tell that he was shocked, as if somebody told him that his dog died. He didn't say a word. He hung up the phone and walked right by me, straight out the door. He didn't tell me where he was going, what he was doing, or when he'd be back.

I heard his vehicle start up and he drove off. Instantly, it dawned on me. He knew.

Hornbuckle was gone for about half an hour. During that time, I was left to wonder if I was just being overly paranoid, or if he really knew. I was nervous and tried to occupy my mind with work. It was no use. Finally, I heard his car pull up and he came back into the office. He didn't say a word to me.

For the rest of the night, Hornbuckle didn't talk to me. I was still wondering if someone had told him about the lawsuit, when one of the hostelers came into the office. He and Hornbuckle started talking loudly. Hornbuckle seemed like he was trying very hard to act as if nothing was wrong.

When he saw that I was looking up, he grabbed at the hosteler's genitals with exaggerated motions. Then, in a purposeful voice dripping with sarcasm, he said, "Oops, I can't do that anymore. That's called sexual harassment."

I left the office certain that Hornbuckle was aware of the lawsuit. I tried to shrug it off and told myself that it was no big deal.

I later found out that the railroad's internal mail had accidentally forwarded the lawsuit to the wrong office. It was sent to the Transportation Department. The Transportation Department opened it, read it, and laid it on the desk for anybody to see. Finally, someone from the office took it to the master mechanic's office, where it belonged.

Pretty soon, word spread like oil in a drip pan. News of my lawsuit was the subject of conversations across the yard all day long before I got there. It was a potentially very hostile situation.

The master mechanic's office was locked that night, but one of Hornbuckle's buddies had a key to the door. He called Hornbuckle (while I was in the office) and told him briefly about the suit. Then, he asked him to drive over and see it for himself.

I disappeared for the rest of the night. I had no choice. No one on the yard would speak to me, least of all my employees. If I got any look at all from the other men on the yard, it was one of loathing. I was rendered powerless as a supervisor. I did the only thing I could think of: I hid on the locomotives.

From the top of the locomotives, I had a bird's-eye view of the office. At one point, Hornbuckle picked up the phone, dialed a number, and spoke for a couple minutes. About ten minutes later, Thomasson walked into the office. He and Hornbuckle talked for about forty-five minutes.

It was an incredibly frightening night for me. As daylight came, Benson came in to work. One of the servicemen asked him how he was doing. "I'm just on hold right now," he told him quietly. I knew that I had stirred up a large and dangerous hornet's nest.

As soon as the shift was over, I hurried over to my truck and left as quickly as I could. I was perspiring and nervous. I felt certain that some of the men were going to jump me and beat the tar out of me. Of course, my anxiety had led me down strange paths before. I was happy to be on my way home and in one piece.

Early the next morning, I called Beverly and told her what had happened. I was furious that the railroad had been so incompetent. She promised to check it out immediately. She told me not to worry, that everything would be all right. If I felt threatened at any time, she wanted me to leave the yard at once. She told me that the next few weeks were not going to be easy, but she would be there for me when I needed her.

The next day I was scheduled to work was the 7th of April, three days after Norfolk Southern received the lawsuit notice from the EEOC. I was as nervous as a fox in a dog kennel. I didn't know what to expect. For all I knew, Hornbuckle and the others were going to jump me in the parking lot and beat the hell out of me. I never got to find out, though, because Beverly called me and told me not to go into work. It seemed that Master Mechanic Mark Bishop and Stephen Stutsman, the Norfolk Southern representative of the EEOC, wanted to meet me and ask me questions.

Marcia and I drove down to Beverly's offices. Haskell Slaughter Young & Johnston occupied an entire floor, 15 or 16 stories up, in a downtown Birmingham high-rise. Mr. Stutsman and Mr. Bishop were waiting in the conference room. Beverly met us out in the lobby and informed me of the situation. She told me to go in to the room and tell them whatever they wanted to know. I was a bit worried when Beverly told me that she wouldn't be joining me. She told me not to sweat it, just tell them the truth.

Marcia and I stepped into the conference room. It was gigantic. An entire wall of picture windows overlooked the city. The conference table, made of a beautiful, dark mahogany, could seat about two dozen people. The room was expensively decorated with plush upholstery on the chairs and ornate carpets. It was a room designed to impress visitors and to intimidate the opposition.

We sat down at the table and I told them everything about Hornbuckle, Thomasson, and Summerlin harassing me, even after I asked them numerous times to stop. I told them about the dead fish in my locker, my extreme weight loss, my medical problems, and my fears.

As they took notes, they assured me that everything was going to be okay. I was skeptical at first. I hadn't seen any results with previous complaints to management.

These men represented powerful offices in Norfolk Southern, so I began to think that maybe they could do something. Maybe they were genuinely concerned. Bishop and Stutsman asked me numerous questions, including names of anyone who might have been a witness to any of the harassment.

During the more graphic stories, Marcia squeezed my hand, willing me to go on. Finally, after a couple hours of conversation, I finished.

Norfolk Southern damage control began. Bishop and Stutsman were major players with the railroad. They were nice enough fellas in the conference room because they needed to be. Both men knew how incredibly damaging my testimony could be. They started treating me like I was their good friend.

Bishop was full of smiles and frowns, whichever was necessary depending on what story I was telling them. He acted like he was just one of the guys. Never mind the fact that I had not once seen him at the yard during third shift, even though it was his job to make sure all of his departments were running smoothly. Now, he was my best buddy. He suggested that we play golf, just the two of us, one day. He also told me that he could have me transferred anywhere I wanted to go on the line. It was my choice. If I ever felt threatened on the yard at night, he would have railroad police assigned to protect me. In short, he was there only to make everything easy for me as a representative of Norfolk Southern.

That very night, Bishop and Stutsman interviewed various other servicemen and attendants on the third shift. They told each man that their conversations would be held completely private. From what I could gather, many of the men talked about Hornbuckle, Thomasson, and Summerlin. The next morning, all three of my harassers were fired.

8

GUIDING LIGHT

Well it was a train that took me away from here
but a train can't bring me home.
—Tom Waits, "Train Song"

Birmingham, Alabama
April 1994

Although my mind was completely focused on my failing health, my nervous disorders, and the lawsuit fiasco at the yard, my heart was totally occupied by Marcia. She was there for me whenever I needed her. I felt horrible that I was not able to provide her with a normal relationship, one with romantic outings, quiet dinners, or weekend trips. She must have seen deep inside me, because she never complained. She loved me for the man I once was and knew I would be again.

I was determined to bring normality to our relationship. Marcia often told me that she was happy being able to take care of me. She told me that it helped her to function. She hated to see me batted around by my co-workers. Instead of feeling sorry for both of us, she made it her mission to help me fight. I wanted to do something for her that was special. I told her what I was thinking and she was game. We did something completely spontaneous right in the midst of my personal war: we got married.

Ever since Marcia and I moved in together, we knew that our search for a life partner was over. All of our previous failed relationships had led up to us finding each other. Now that the hard part of finding each other was over, we needed only to decide where the "happily ever after" part fit in to our story. Unfortunately for both of us, my situation at work was blocking those plans.

After I committed to the lawsuit, Marcia and I had a long talk about our future. I told her what the lawsuit meant regarding our lives together. I knew that I would eventually lose my job. I would be subjected to all sorts of ridicule, especially because I was charging other men with sexual harassment. That was a first, as far as I'd heard. It was going to be a long and painful journey, especially if we went to court. Other people would ask about the lawsuit with morbid fascination. I was embarrassed and ashamed, but I knew that I had to take it on no matter the consequences.

Marcia understood that I wasn't after money. My pride wouldn't let Hornbuckle, Thomasson, and Summerlin get away with the things they'd done. But beyond that, I didn't want anyone else to have to go through what I did. When Marcia told me that she wanted to stand by my side through it all – the ridicule, the embarrassment, and the heartache – we knew that the commitment was strong with both of us. We were bonded together. Marcia and I decided to laugh in the face of the chaos that was our lives by getting married.

On the day before Bishop and Stutsman came to town, Marcia and I drove down to Chattanooga, Tennessee. We found out that a marriage could be arranged and completed in one day there. It was a very difficult trip for me, because I didn't like to stray too far from our home. Anything unfamiliar made me nervous. Marcia told me not to worry, that she would be with me the entire time.

We set off towards Chattanooga at around noon on April 6th. We knew that no blood tests were required and that marriage licenses were easily obtained. There was an hour time difference in Chattanooga that we hadn't considered, so by the time we got there we had gained an hour and it was pouring rain. We arrived at around 5 P.M., right when the courts were closing. While I frantically filled out paperwork for a marriage license, Marcia found a payphone. We needed a judge who would marry us and Marcia kept dialing number after number.

Finally, Marcia got lucky. A judge told her that he would stay late to marry us if we really wanted. We brought other clothes, but didn't have time to change into them. I grabbed Marcia's hand and we ran down the street to the courthouse, the marriage license protected under my jacket. It was still pouring rain, and by the time we arrived at the courthouse, we were soaking wet.

The judge was a very nice, older man. He invited us into his chambers and sat us down. We chatted for a while and told him a little about our relationship and how we'd met. He told us that it was a joy for him to deal with two people who wanted to get married so badly that they braved the interstates and rain. He had spent the day dealing with people who wanted to

A rare moment of pleasure during the ordeal. Eddie and Marcia Martin on their wedding day in Chattanooga, Tennessee, April 6, 1995.

be divorced. In a few short minutes, and after his signature was placed on the license, Marcia and I were officially man and wife.

I talked Marcia into visiting the famous Chattanooga Choo-Choo while we were in town. We ate and then drove over to Market Street where the Terminal Station sits. The station was built in 1909 for Southern Railway, and the interior was fashioned after a well-known New York bank. In 1970, after Southern Railway stopped its service to Chattanooga and the terminal was on the verge of being torn down, the city restored the complex. It is now a registered National Historic Site.

We strolled through the station and I again felt connected to my ancestors who had worked for Southern Railway. There were no unhappy memories in Chattanooga. I felt alive and happy for the first time in a long time as my new wife and I held hands and walked through the historic grounds. We had our picture taken on the steps of the train made famous by the Glenn Miller Orchestra. We felt like children as we kissed our way through the park.

Perhaps it was the memory of this perfect evening that helped me deal with the mess back in Birmingham. After Hornbuckle, Thomasson, and Summerlin were fired, I felt instant relief, but dreaded any backlash or revenge these men might take against me. Over the next few weeks, I would come to rely heavily on the memories of the time Marcia and I spent in Chattanooga and the happiness we felt there.

The good times were few and far between. Though I had medical attention with Dr. Toliver, it did not cover all of my ailments. My body and mind were falling apart from the inside out. I was sick on so many levels.

Not only could I not concentrate on my work anymore, I was frightened to death of going to work. Even after my harassers were dismissed, I found myself looking over my shoulder every ten seconds for fear that I was about to be attacked. It was an uneasy feeling to always fear the bogey man, even in the light of day. Unlike the children of the world who grew up

The newlyweds

and dismissed their monsters as superstition, I knew that mine lived and breathed.

Except for the day that Dr. Toliver had given me a tranquilizer shot, I was still not sleeping. My long hours and physical work made no difference. The nightmares were constant. Hornbuckle and Thomasson were as much a part of my dreams as they were in my waking life. I woke up drenched in sweat every couple of hours, positive that my dreams and reality had somehow merged. Marcia was always there to tell me that I was only dreaming. It was that much more difficult to fall asleep, knowing that as soon as sleep took hold of me, the nightmares would once again seize my mind.

People made me nervous. The cry of a small child, a packed elevator, and grocery store lines gave me anxiety. There was no logical reason for my anxieties, but in my mind they were very real.

I had gone from a social person to a complete recluse in just three months. My free time was spent indoors. Marcia had to do all of the shopping and errands. Except for my anxiety-ridden drive to work, she became my only link to the outside world.

I picked up two destructive ways to cope with my ordeals. I began smoking for the first time in my life, and I started to drink heavily. Alcohol seemed to help me fall asleep and to cope with what was going on. I drank up to eight beers a day. The cigarettes seemed to calm my nerves, even though I knew they were not a real cure. I cursed myself for picking up the habit after having said "no" all of my life.

Through it all, my wife stuck by my side. We attempted to overcome my impotence, but it was no use. She tried to get me to go places with her. At the last minute I'd literally beg to stay home. She tried to get me to talk about my innermost thoughts and fears, but I felt that she might somehow be infected if I told her everything. She knew what had been done to me. She knew the surface. There was much that she didn't know and something had to be done about it.

I followed Dr. Toliver's advice and decided to seek counseling. I called the insurance company that I used for my railroad medical coverage and asked them about any approved counselors in the area. They gave me a name and I made an appointment. I was nervous about going to a therapist. I didn't want to start talking about my father and my childhood and other areas that I didn't think were relevant. Grudgingly, I drove to the office of Harriet Schaffer.

Ms. Schaffer was a licensed professional counselor who primarily worked with families. We sat down in her office and began our conversation with a brief background of myself. I told her where I was from, how long I had worked for the railroad, how many siblings I had, and other such things. Slowly, she brought the conversation around to why I felt I needed counseling. I opened my mind to her and let her inside. She was horrified and told me so.

She had never heard of anything like what had been done to me. I explained to her my anxieties and physical ailments. She told me that if I continued to expose myself to those situations, I could have a mental breakdown. The statement scared me, but it confirmed where I felt I was heading.

After three visits with Ms. Schaffer, she determined that I was suffering from generalized anxiety disorder, which is merely a catchall phrase that took into account all of my symptoms. I found it helpful to talk about my problems, but I felt that she spent too much time going over my family background. I realized that forming a background on a patient was necessary, but she seemed to look for answers in my past, rather than in my present. I wanted her to offer suggestions on how to control some of my anxieties and deal with my irrational fears.

Meanwhile, I was not doing well at work. I had trouble concentrating and dealing with the other servicemen. Even a change to second shift didn't help. The men were hostile towards me for breaking up the "family." A few days after my marriage, I told master mechanic Bishop that I was going on vacation for a couple weeks. He told me that I needed it.

Marcia and I drove down to Panama City, Florida. It felt great to get out of Birmingham. It was a makeshift honeymoon, a time for us to celebrate our marriage. It was not a traditional honeymoon, though. While we were there, we didn't go to the beach every day, we didn't go out to eat, or even see any sights. We mostly stayed in the hotel room for two weeks.

The only other person who knew of our whereabouts was Beverly Baker. I had called her and told her that Marcia and I needed some time away from the hostility of Birmingham.

It *was* a nice vacation from our worries. I didn't see a single train or talk to any railroad officials while we were there. I managed to get a little color back in my skin from the Florida sun while we sat by the pool. As I looked over at Marcia, I couldn't help but think that I had finally found the love of my life. The fact that she had endured so much with me and still wanted to stick around was proof enough in my book.

When we finally got back to Birmingham, I felt that I was a little more prepared for work. I was wrong. On April 28, I went back to working second shift at the diesel shop, and my fellow servicemen greeted me with the silent treatment. I was now an outsider. No one would speak to me or even look in my direction. They pretended that I didn't exist. I began getting crank phone calls in the office. When I answered, the caller would hang up.

I was startled when master mechanic Bishop waved me over to his car one night and invited me to take a drive with him. As we drove around, we chatted about how things were going for me. I told him flat out that nobody listened to or even acknowledged my existence. He didn't seem surprised.

Bishop next told me something that made me very angry. Apparently, the unions had become involved after Hornbuckle, Thomasson, and Summerlin were dismissed. The representatives from the Electricians and the Firemen and Oilers unions began talking to many of the servicemen who had witnessed some of my harassment. Consequently, Bishop warned me, many of the witnesses were changing their stories. It was turning into a union versus management issue.

Bishop continued to explain to me that he wanted to fix the

problem. Anything I needed from him he would do. He told me again about police protection and a transfer to the yard of my choice. He said that he was going to do everything possible to correct my working environment. I told him that I was frightened to even be there on the yard.

That same day, I got a phone call from my old golfing buddy, Eddie Hickman, who worked on the railroad in Spartanburg. He told me that news of my lawsuit and the problems in Birmingham had spread all over the railroad. I was the talk of Norfolk Southern. Hickman's boss had even asked Eddie what my sexual preference was.

Eddie had also heard things from others while at a training camp for Norfolk Southern. Situated in southern South Carolina, the camp was known as "The Forest." The railroad owned thousands of acres of land that the bigwigs used for fishing and hunting. Eddie had been invited down. Sitting at a table with other railroad personnel, he learned that one of the men was a general foreman from Birmingham. The conversation turned to me and my lawsuit. The foreman told the group of people around the table that he knew there was something wrong with me the minute he shook my hand. Eddie stood up for me, telling the man that he had better shut his mouth.

I was being portrayed as the bad guy all the way across the tracks. Whether they labeled me a troublemaker or a homosexual, it didn't matter. My reputation was ruined. Even if I did accept a transfer, the working conditions wouldn't be much different than those in Birmingham. The railroad was like a fraternity and I was a wayward brother. Wherever I went, I would not be treated fairly. My days with the railroad were numbered.

On April 29, Bishop called me at the office and told me that he had heard some people making threats about me. I was alarmed. He told me to take a few days off and he'd start me on first shift when I returned the next week. I went home relieved. I wasn't getting much work done anyway. None of the men followed my directions.

I started work on first shift on May 3. Because general foreman Benson had failed to act on my complaints, he had been demoted and transferred. There was a new general foreman on duty that morning when I reported in for work. He told me to stay in the office for the entire shift. I felt eyes on me the whole time I was there. I had been working for about an hour when the new general foreman told me to go on home. He said that my presence was throwing off the workload and that they didn't really need me there.

I had finally arrived at the end. I was not officially fired, nor was I told that I wouldn't be working for the railroad anymore. But I knew. I knew that was the end of my railroad career. My fellow workers had banished me to the outside world, never to return. That day, Ms. Schaffer wrote a letter to railroad officials, and I officially went on indefinite medical leave.

I was mentally unprepared for the dismissal. I panicked and didn't know what I was going to do for a living. My livelihood was gone. I had worked for the railroad the past fifteen years. It was all that I knew how to do. Not that I was old, but I worried over starting a new career from the bottom rung. There was nothing I could think of that I wanted more than to work with the locomotives of my childhood fantasies.

I was still being paid, but that did nothing to relieve the pain I felt. Marcia was happy that I didn't have to go back to the yard. She worried every time I went into work, especially after news of the lawsuit was released. She and I spent all of our free time together.

She took it upon herself to guide my therapy. Her first step was to take the crutch of alcohol away from me. Rather than allow me to sit in front of the television for hours on end while drinking beer after beer, she made me perform various tasks around the house. I worked in the yard a little and fixed a few things in the house which needed attention. She kept my mind occupied with other things.

My wife also monitored my eating habits. I probably would

have withered away had she not made me eat double helpings of meat and potatoes. I even began barbecuing again, one of my preferred pastimes and my favorite way to cook. I consider it an art form and it's something I'm very good at. I concentrated on getting the coals and the wood chips exactly right. Slowly, I gained a little of my weight back. Even with a nervous stomach and not much of an appetite, I found it difficult to turn down slow-cooked barbecue.

Marcia was better than any of the medications prescribed to me by Dr. Toliver and Ms. Schaffer. Sure, the pills they had me taking helped control my panic attacks and my sleeplessness, but they were no cure for my depression. Marcia was the only cure I knew of. She had stuck by me when I thought no one would.

Through our talks, Marcia helped me realize certain truths about the railroad. It was difficult to go up against. The organization operated through intimidation and fear, just as Hornbuckle and Thomasson had. It had been less difficult for me to withdraw and blame myself. She likened the railroad to an elephant in the living room. It was easier to walk around the problem than get rid of it. Fear was something that the railroad instilled in all of its employees. I had been taught to ignore my gut feelings, which made me sick with stress. I felt like I had no choices.

As I was recovering, Norfolk Southern was preparing for battle. I was too busy trying to repair my own little world to notice. Now that I wasn't working at the railroad, I was out of the loop. I was concentrating fully on my new marriage and less and less on my problems. In a few short days, though, all of my old wounds were about to be re-opened.

9

FROM INSULT TO INJURY

Birmingham, Alabama
April 1994

N orfolk Southern went from provider to strained acquain-
tance in no time at all. The railway company was like a
disagreeable relative that I invited over for a holiday meal.
I grudgingly acknowledged that it was a part of my life, yet I
didn't want to have anything to do with it. I knew that in order
to see the lawsuit through, I had to cooperate with the company that had betrayed me. There would be questions, investigations, and depositions before it was all over. I knew all about
that. What I didn't know was how dirty they would fight.

I had lost my way of life, but found my true love. It wasn't a
bad trade-off for me. Still, I missed working on the locomotives that fed my family for three generations. Looking back,
Birmingham was a bust. I could have picked Roanoke or
Danville and the nightmare probably would never have happened. I cursed Norfolk Southern for giving me the choice
that led to my downfall.

While on indefinite medical leave of absence, I mentally
prepared for the lawsuit. During the last month I worked, I
wrote my thoughts down in a makeshift journal. I documented

what Hornbuckle and Thomasson had done to me. I found it comforting to write down what was going on. It almost put me outside of the action. In reality, though, I knew that I was not an observer, but a victim. Still, it helped to see my thoughts organized on the page before me, especially when I found it difficult to think rationally.

When Hornbuckle, Thomasson, Summerlin, and Benson were fired or demoted, there was no formal investigation by the railroad into the allegations. The railroad merely interviewed various employees about the charges I made. Apparently, there was sufficient corroboration of my story to merit the actions they took against the men. The railroad had moved or fired the men as a damage control attempt.

Now, however, Norfolk Southern decided to hold formal investigations into my allegations. There were no depositions and no one was sworn in. The people involved in the investigations were allowed to have their lawyers present. I was required to be in attendance.

By this time, trial lawyer Stephen Poer joined my legal team. Steve was the most brilliant attorney I had ever encountered. He could cite cases and legal precedents at the drop of a hat. Yet he didn't look like a high-powered lawyer from *L.A. Law*. But beneath his unassuming appearance lurked a shrewd mind. His coming on board told me that this case was definitely going to trial.

The first formal investigation, that for Preston Thomasson, took place on April 18, 1994. Lawrence Smith, Norfolk Southern's Director of Mechanical Facilities and Training, presided as the hearing officer.

I was in no shape to attend the hearing, though they asked me by letter to make myself available. After a few hours of arguments, denials, and confusion, Smith allowed for a postponement until I could attend. I wasn't comfortable attending an investigation into any of my attackers, especially if they were in attendance, but on May 5, I drove to the motel with Marcia and Steve Poer. They were not allowed into the proceedings, but the railroad supplied them with a room where they could wait for me.

During the first set of interviews with Thomasson, he and the union provided witnesses for his case. Included were Curtis Brierly, Tom Burgay, and Charles Rice.

While I was at home in dire straits, these men told lies to the investigators. They denied having seen anything out of the ordinary go on between Thomasson and myself. They did admit to casual horseplay, but nothing that would construe actual "sexual harassment." They had changed their stories dramatically since that first night when Bishop and Stutsman interviewed them. They went from being witnesses for me to people with selective memories. It seemed that the unions had strong persuasion techniques.

I was angry when I found out that the men had changed their stories, but Bishop had warned me this would happen. I really couldn't blame the men. They still needed to feed their families. No one in his right mind would want to back me up, especially in such a tight-knit group as the railroad. I was a whistle-blower and therefore subject to ridicule and whispers.

The union probably told them that if they supported me, they would find it difficult to work for Norfolk Southern afterward. The union played dirty and I was left alone, my word against theirs.

When I entered the motel room, I saw union representatives, Bishop, Thomasson, Smith, and a tape recorder. It was already 8 P.M. and I expected a long night ahead. After a few preliminary inquiries, the union representatives began asking pointed questions about the actions that Thomasson was being accused of. I went into detail and never faltered. I repeated the exact accounts I'd given Marcia, my attorneys, Bishop, Stutsman, and my doctors. I remembered everything. As I told the men in the room about the horrors inflicted upon me, I felt anxious and nervous. I relived those nights of terror with every description.

In addition to my other physical symptoms, I also suffered

from chronic diarrhea. It was a result of my lack of appetite and nervousness. I never felt more uncomfortable in my life. I could hardly sit still for more than an hour before having to rush into the bathroom. It was embarrassing and painful. My bowels felt as if they were on fire. Having to tell the horrible stories over and over again didn't help matters.

I resented the fact that I had to attend these investigations. In a perfect world, I decided, a man wouldn't have to prove himself when he was so obviously the victim. A person could look at the facts and decide for himself.

In earlier testimonies given to Bishop and Stutsman, fellow employees verified much of my testimony. Now, the whole process was repeated for the benefit of the union representatives. It wasn't fair, especially now that the witnesses were changing their stories.

I was asked about pamphlets that I supposedly received in my paycheck envelopes. One had to do with reporting sexual harassment and the proper procedure in doing so. The other had to do with disciplinary procedures.

I honestly could not remember having laid eyes on any pamphlets. Usually, when receiving a paycheck, I took out the check and threw the rest away. It was like a utility bill. There were always advertisements in those envelopes about how to save energy and suggestions for cooling your house in the summer. To me, those advertisements were merely packing around the important thing: the bill. The same went for my paycheck. If the pamphlets on sexual harassment and discipline were really important, the railroad would have made me sign a form saying I'd read and understood them.

I was asked why I didn't place a disciplinary letter in Thomasson's file. He was, after all, my subordinate. They didn't seem to understand that though he was "officially" my subordinate, he and Hornbuckle were tight. I told the investigators that I discussed matters with Hornbuckle, my supervisor. If I attempted to discipline Thomasson, Hornbuckle would have made things even more uncomfortable for me, if such a thing were possible. Hornbuckle called Thomasson "his boy." Who was I to go against that?

Mr. Smith was very fair in his presiding. He often asked me to clarify points or explain things that he wasn't clear on. He seemed to genuinely want to get to the bottom of the case. I got the feeling that he didn't much care for the union representatives. He didn't allow them to walk all over me when they attempted to do so. Smith also didn't give them too much freedom in their line of questioning. He asked them what many questions had to do with the case at hand.

I left the motel at eleven that night. Not once did I consult Steve. He told me before I went into the investigation to merely tell the truth. If I stuck to the truth, no harm could come to me. I hoped he was right. After three hours of testimony, I felt drained, and Marcia and I rushed home. The next formal investigation, that of Hornbuckle, was scheduled in one week. I was most nervous about that one.

At noon on May 12, 1994, I arrived at the motel for the investigation into Hornbuckle. In addition to the people present for the earlier investigation, Hornbuckle had more witnesses. Thomasson and Summerlin showed up as character references for him. I couldn't understand the logic to that. To me, that was like having Adolph Hitler and Genghis Khan testifying on Satan's behalf. Besides, both Thomasson and Summerlin had been fired. I smelled a rat and knew that all three of my attackers had discussed strategies, although they would never admit to it.

During Hornbuckle's investigation, each of the eighteen charges filed by my attorneys and me was read through, first with Bishop, then with me. Because Bishop had interviewed Hornbuckle about the eighteen charges shortly after they were filed, he had direct knowledge of Hornbuckle's initial responses. Hornbuckle admitted to Bishop that he had asked to see my penis, offered to show his, and called me and others the "AIDS Three."

Bishop also wrote down the names of employees who had

verified the charges during his questioning. It seemed like an open and shut case, but the union reps wanted to go through it all again, especially after having "talked" to my witnesses.

For the first time in the investigations, the subject of sexual harassment was brought up. It was during a round of questioning between Hornbuckle's union rep and Bishop. The representative asked Bishop if both Hornbuckle and I were male individuals. Bishop answered "yes."

"And you're charging [Hornbuckle] with sexual harassment towards Mr. Martin?" asked the union representative.

"Sexual harassment does not recognize gender," replied Bishop.

Then, Bishop and the rep discussed what constituted sexual harassment. Bishop told those present that Norfolk Southern's policy allowed that the company "accepts the Equal Employment Opportunity Commission's definition of sexual harassment as unwelcome sexual advances, requests for sexual favors, and other verbal or physical conduct of a sexual nature when submission to such conduct is made either explicitly or implicitly a term or condition of an individual's employment."

The union rep made a big deal out of the fact that both Hornbuckle and I were heterosexual men. To the union man, a heterosexual man could not sexually harass another heterosexual man. It was not possible, just as it was not possible for one white person to discriminate against another white person for being white.

In my eyes, though, Hornbuckle's actions were a form of sexual harassment. He told me that if I didn't allow the men to grope me, I would be fired. There was no gray area there.

I was called in for questioning, and they asked me to read through the charges and verify whether or not they were true. I read through each of the charges and testified (though none of us were put under oath) that all of the charges made were accurate. Because Smith already had my testimony from Thomasson's investigation, I didn't have to tell the entire story again. I was dismissed at that time, but told to stay at the motel in case I was needed.

Later in the day when Hornbuckle was questioned, he made himself out to be the victim. He was ready with an explanation for each and every charge, facts be damned. For example, when Smith asked him about calling two other men and me the "Three Muske-Queers," he stated that we heard incorrectly, that he only called us the "Three Musketeers." The same went for his AIDS taunts. Hornbuckle told the panel that he was worried about another worker and asked him "you're getting mighty skinny, you ain't got that AIDS somebody said [you do]?"

He was blameless according to his testimony, and he had no idea what my motivation was in perpetuating such a false case against him. Thomasson and Summerlin backed up his stories.

Ironically, the investigation into Summerlin, the man who did the least amount of disreputable things to me (besides occasional taunts and exposing his tatoo), lasted longer by far than the previous two. It spanned twelve hours, between 7 A.M. and 7 P.M., on May 18, 1994. His union rep wanted everything spelled out again "for the record." Master mechanic Bishop was under the gun more than I was during the questioning.

The union representative made Bishop go over each and every detail of his preliminary questions with Summerlin before he fired him. Summerlin's statements from that night, such as "You know who to play with and who not to play with" and "I am guilty of horseplay," were entered into the record. Luckily, Bishop had made detailed notes during his initial questioning of all three harassers. He relied on them that day.

Once again, there were the usual suspects standing up as character witnesses. As had happened at both Thomasson's and Hornbuckle's investigations, my witnesses took back their incriminating remarks and shifted the blame over to me. I was made out to be an incompetent fool who couldn't get along with the other men nor do my job correctly.

I felt severely betrayed by my subordinates. But, as they say, "all's fair in love and war," and I was definitely at war.

After two weeks of investigations, I felt anything but relief. If anything, I felt much the same as I did when I worked at the yard and was being harassed. The investigations undid my feelings of relaxation of the past couple weeks, and I was once again on edge and full of anxiety. I didn't think the situation or my lawsuit would ever get resolved. Neither did I think that I would ever feel better as long as I stayed in Birmingham.

Marcia and I got many crank phone calls at the house. There were no direct threats. The caller would merely hang up the phone whenever we answered. It was incredibly annoying and sometimes pretty scary.

I received a desperate call from Hornbuckle's wife, pleading with me to do something about the charges I'd made. She told me that she was frightened of what her husband might do. I didn't know how to take that one – either he might try to harm himself, or he might try to harm me. Either way, I didn't like hearing the message.

For the next month, I did very little but stick around the house. Marcia worked while I took care of the household duties. Though Birmingham was a great city, it held too many painful memories. I couldn't help but associate the city with my troubles. I was determined to get better, no matter what it took. I discussed the matter with Marcia and we made up our minds. We decided to move to South Carolina.

❖   ❖

On June 23, 1994, Marcia and I packed up a U-Haul trailer with as much stuff as we could carry. We rented the house in Gardendale, so we were able to leave without worries. With the dog in the car and our bags packed, we set off towards South Carolina, my lifelong home. As we drove out of Birmingham, I felt a profound sense of relief. It was like a glimpse of the sun after a six-month rainy season.

Back home in Greenville, Marcia and I moved into the house I had been building for the past few years. It was the perfect therapy to get my mind off of my worries. There was much to do to complete our home. I set about completing the drywall and installing plumbing fixtures in the interior. It felt good to work with my hands again. As I completed each project, much like the work I did for the railroad, I looked back on the job with a sense of accomplishment. I once again felt productive.

We didn't want for money. Technically, I was still employed by Norfolk Southern and on indefinite sick leave. The company allowed its employees to take medical leave for up to six months. After the six-month period, you either had to go on some type of disability or the company terminated you. Norfolk Southern wanted me to come back to work in Birmingham at the same position, but even my doctors advised against it in writing. Dr. Toliver said that I should never go back to work for a company that allowed such appalling harassment to go on.

When I left Birmingham, I also left Dr. Toliver and Ms. Schaffer behind. That meant that I needed to find a medical doctor who could monitor my physical recovery and a counselor who could help me deal with the mental and emotional issues. Once again, I went through the railroad insurance company to get the names of doctors. Part of me hated having to rely on the railroad for anything. The other part of me was grateful that my medical bills were still covered by the same company that helped cause my problems.

My general practitioner, Dr. Wallace, was mostly concerned with my weight and nervous disposition. He prescribed a high-protein diet and sedatives. I saw him about twice a month for check-ups. He was a no-nonsense doctor and not as personally offended by what happened to me as Dr. Toliver had been. Still, I was glad that he seemed concerned about me.

Whereas Ms. Schaffer hadn't offered much in the way of techniques for controlling my anxieties, my new counselor

Eddie working on his house. Along with other medical problems, he lost over thirty-five pounds as a result of the harassment.

taught me some wonderful exercises. Dr. Kathleen Robbins was a certified psychotherapist and a remarkable woman. It was not getting any easier for me to tell my story, even after having told it so many times already. I was shy with Dr. Robbins at first. I was embarrassed to tell her about being sexually harassed. On our first session, I went through the basics without discussing the specifics.

I explained my self-imposed isolation. I couldn't go to the hardware store without having panic attacks. Standing amidst a store full of strangers made me nervous. I didn't want to turn my back on any of the patrons for fear that one of them would attack me from behind. Anybody seemed like a potential attacker. The scary thing was that I knew these were irrational thoughts but was helpless to stop them.

I told Dr. Robbins about my physical troubles and my inability to fall asleep. She listened attentively and didn't rush me when I was talking. She was very easy-going and let me get to things at my own pace. I felt a little more relaxed after each session with her. It was different talking to Dr. Robbins than it was with Marcia. My wife helped me more than any doctor ever could, but Dr. Robbins was able to diagnose exactly what was wrong with me and put it into clinical terms. For some reason, I needed to hear that my behavior was normal for someone who had been through what I had. I needed to be sure that I was not alone.

Dr. Robbins' initial finding was that I suffered from "adjustment disorder with mixed emotional features." She saw that I was having difficulty adjusting to life without the railroad. She understood that the most difficult aspect of losing my job was that I had been forced to leave by circumstances I was powerless to control. Most importantly, she showed me how to relax when I felt anxious.

In order to help me overcome my fear of crowds, Dr. Robbins suggested I attempt going out more often. I was supposed to go to places that wouldn't pose a threat to me. Eventually, she said, it would get easier to be in public places. She also worked on improving my self-esteem and feelings of self-worth through various exercises and discussions. Thanks to her efforts along with Marcia's enthusiastic approach to my getting healthy, I honestly began to feel better.

After numerous sessions, Dr. Robbins changed her initial diagnosis to that of post-traumatic stress disorder (PTSD). She found that my stress was such that it might take a long time to work through. With PTSD, there is sufficient trauma rendered to make the patient have extreme anxiety for lengthy periods of time. The continued episodes of sexual harassment had a lasting effect on my emotional state. It didn't help matters that I still had a lawsuit to work through. Every time I thought about the lawsuit, it was a reminder of what I had endured.

The lawsuit would result in an eventual court date, especially after a rapid offer of settlement by Norfolk Southern. In late June, the railroad sent my attorneys a letter with a cash settlement offer of $25,000 to drop the lawsuit and come back to work. This was extremely insulting. They didn't seem to realize that I was unable to come back to work. I would be a basket case working in the place where I was harassed.

It was never about the money. I knew that I needed to go to court so that I could prove that I was right. That was a big step towards regaining my pride. It made my blood boil that Norfolk Southern tried to buy my silence with such a small figure. I wanted them to pay – both with money and with any negative publicity that resulted from their negligence. I wanted to make sure that no one else would go through what I did. Only then would I feel like I'd won.

10

STRESS FOR SUCCESS?

Greenville, South Carolina
November 1994

was officially fired from the railroad in November 1994. Every month, as a condition of my medical leave of absence from the railroad, Dr. Robbins wrote a letter to the railroad's medical department. In the letters, she told the department that I was not mentally able to come back to work in Birmingham. I was allowed up to six months. On October 24, 1994, almost six months after I'd left Norfolk Southern, a letter arrived telling me either to report back to work or be terminated.

"Are you willing and able to go back to work, Eddie?" Marcia asked me in her no-nonsense tone of voice.

"No. You know that," I told her.

"Then don't. We both knew there was no way you could go back. We'll make it right, though. We'll be all right, too," she told me.

From the moment of my termination, Norfolk Southern treated me as if I'd declared war on them. I was not the happy little camper they expected. In a company where men left their families in the lurch for months at a time if the railroad called, I was something they hadn't counted on. If they were surprised,

96

they didn't let on. Instead, they began to fight back, throwing the rules of the game out the window. The railroad company was out for blood – my blood – and they seemed set to get it however they could.

Norfolk Southern was like Mike Tyson in the ring: they knew they were losing, so they went for broke. I knew that I was in for a tough battle when they contacted my first wife – and mother to my children – the first week of November 1994.

She and her husband were sitting down for a quiet Friday evening when the telephone rang. Her husband answered. The caller identified himself as the director of audit for Norfolk Southern. The caller asked to speak to my ex-wife, but because it was late in the evening, her husband asked what he wanted. The Norfolk Southern man briefly told him about my situation and wanted confirmation on something he'd "heard" – did I expose myself to one of my children in June of 1991?

My ex-wife's husband told the caller in no uncertain terms that they wanted nothing to do with him or the lawsuit. Furthermore, he told the man, if Norfolk Southern continued to call, he would do whatever was necessary to end the harassment. After he hung up, he called me and told me about it. Then he wrote a letter to my attorneys outlining the call.

Beverly and Steve discussed filing a defamation suit against the caller, but decided against it. They knew better than I how a caged animal strikes out at anything within its reach.

❖   ❖

The next year and a half crept by for Marcia and me. They were months filled with stress. I was given a regular dose of sedatives and counseling sessions – more of the former and less of the latter. The nightmares continued, but I was assured that they were normal. There was no way to control what the mind did when left on its own during the night. I finally seemed to be getting a hold of my emotions, though I still had flashes of humiliation and anger. Dr. Robbins gave me excellent advice on how to calm myself down when I felt threatened or anxious.

I continued work on our house, which sat on a wooded, five-acre lot. After a couple years of building it myself, it was coming together nicely. I laid all the tiles in the kitchen myself and put up the cabinetry. It gave me a tremendous sense of satisfaction to step back and look at what I'd accomplished. While the house was under construction, Marcia and I lived in a smaller house on the property that I planned to rent out later. We were very happy and I thought that things seemed normal again. Then, the floor fell out beneath my feet.

I was so wrapped up in myself all those months that I never paused to see how any of this was affecting Marcia. She took all of my pain and misery upon herself and absorbed it in hopes that she could better help me. She was such a fighter during those long months of abuse. All she cared about was that the man she loved got better. I never noticed her sleepless nights or her bouts of depression. I should have paid her more attention.

It was late afternoon, and I left for the hardware store to get additional materials for the house. A friend of mine was doing some finishing work on the house when Marcia walked down. I got back from the store and my friend cornered me at the car. He told me that Marcia was speaking incoherently, not making any sense at all. One look at my friend's face told me he was not joking.

When I went to her, she began accusing me of having an affair with a woman named Janet Green. She talked about meeting Emilio Estevez and Charlie Sheen in a restaurant the night before and how they'd spent the night in our house. She looked at the unpainted walls in the house and told me the color was all wrong. She was hysterical.

I was scared and didn't know what to do. I called Dr. Robbins. Marcia had been with me to see her a few times to deal with some of the stress she was feeling — stress that, it seemed, had finally taken its toll on her. Dr. Robbins told me to drive her to a nearby residential psychiatric center immediately.

When I got there, I told the attendant what was happening to my wife. She walked over to the delusional Marcia and talked with her. Suddenly, Marcia lost it. She began speaking off-the-wall and having hallucinations. The attendant called for help, and it took five people to hold Marcia down. I was out of my mind watching my wife in such pain. The staff decided to rush her to Marshall Pickens, a mental health institute. Somehow, they convinced me to drive home. They would contact me when they knew more.

When Marcia got to Pickens, she began talking nonsense to the nurse. She told her that I ran off with Janet Green and took her truck and the furniture. She wanted the police called immediately. They sedated her and called me instead. When they asked me who Janet Green was, I told them I had no idea. Later, we found out that Janet Green was a character on one of Marcia's favorite soap operas.

My wife was assigned a psychiatrist for her next two weeks at the institute. I visited whenever I could. Over those few days, the doctor diagnosed Marcia as manic-depressive; she had a bipolar disorder. Doctors believe that bipolar disorders are caused by imbalances of brain chemicals called neurotransmitters. Neurotransmitters act as the brain's electrical mood regulating system, and a manic episode, such as the one Marcia had, is brought on by a lack of these regulators. It is a genetic disease that often rears its head during highly stressful times.

Marcia was put on prescriptions of lithium and about ten other medications. Later, Dr. Robbins took her off many of them. She was taken off of lithium and put on Depakote® a sodium-based medication mined in the Carolinas that has been found to prevent manic episodes.

She began to feel better after those first couple weeks. I realized how delicate health could be. Marcia was one of the most important people in my life, and I never wanted to lose her. I thanked God that, with medication, her condition could be controlled. A few days later, my insurance coverage and wages ran out with the railroad.

I knew that I needed to find work, especially after I had to sell two of my six rental properties to pay the bills. The trouble was that I still hated crowds. There wasn't much I could do that wouldn't put me in contact with a large number of people. I was very insecure and felt safe only when isolated. It scared me to go out looking for a job. All I really knew how to do well was railroad work. Anxiety stepped in, brought about by my lack of employment, and I could barely pick up the want ads for the fear.

Marcia suggested that since I liked cars so much, why not check the want ads for a car salesman position? I remembered my mother telling me when I was younger and always tinkering with drag cars, "If you can't do anything else, you can always sell cars." I figured that a car dealership was a good place to start.

I would only have to deal with one or two people at a time in that situation and I decided it wouldn't be too stressful for me. I drove over to Bradshaw Automotive in Greer, not too far from the house. After an interview, I got the job and began working at selling cars.

I was a car salesman for about three months and did fairly well, although I had problems on the job, too. I was prone to anxiety attacks, but I made myself go on. I was never a quitter. I could never tell when I was going to have an attack. Once, I sat at a desk talking to a prospective customer. The deal was falling apart before me and I started to panic. My heart raced and my face became flushed. I got to the point where I couldn't even write.

But I forced myself through the attacks (as Dr. Robbins taught me) and I sold many cars. It was never going to make us a proper living, though, and at the end of the month I barely had enough money to pay the bills.

After three months of selling cars for a disappointing pay-check, I went to speak with the sales manager. The clincher was a commission check for $300 after selling eleven cars. I told the sales manager that I'd be better off on unemployment. He liked my work ethic and didn't want to see me leave. He fetched the general manager of the facility, and we all sat in the office to discuss my situation. The GM told me that I was a real professional and offered me $500 on the spot to stay.

"Well, that's not going to help me next month, " I told him.

The GM wanted to know if I was interested in working in the service department. He felt my personality would be well suited to a position there.

I accepted the job with regular hours and a regular salary. There would be no more living paycheck to paycheck, stressing about whether or not I would sell a car and make a commission. I went to work in the service department as a service writer, the guy that writes up the paperwork on a car needing repairs and sends it on into the shop.

I was still having problems with the anxiety. It was a high stress job where some customers got extremely upset about repairs to their car and took their anger out on me. I considered it a form of therapy, though. After I got through each confrontation, I felt a little better about myself. I worked through my problems with determination.

I was chugging along in a comfortable manner when Steve Poer and Beverly Baker called me back to Birmingham. They needed me to answer questions at a deposition before the trial. It seemed that all I had been doing lately was answering questions. Lawyers for Norfolk Southern, Hornbuckle, and Summerlin had me fill out questionnaires called interrogatories. The questions ranged from background information to clarification of the charges filed.

On September 24, 1995, I sat down in the conference room at Haskell Slaughter Young & Johnston with my attorneys, Norfolk Southern counsel, Hornbuckle, Thomasson, Summerlin, and their attorneys. Steve and Beverly told me to relax and answer each question truthfully and fully. Then we entered the conferene room.

It was a routine pre-trial deposition and part of a process known as "discovery," where the lawyers for the defendants found out what there was to know about me. It seemed to me like an invasion of privacy – one of my charges against the defendants – but I had to go along with it. Hardly any of the questions I'd been asked before had anything at all to do with the fact that I'd been sexually harassed. I was duly sworn in and told that this was all "on the record."

We began the proceedings at nine in the morning. Surveying the room, including the court reporter and myself, I counted thirteen people present. Out of that number, ten were on the opposing team. It was an extremely stressful situation, having to sit there with the three men who sexually harassed me and their team of cutthroat attorneys. Once again, I felt overpowered and exposed. I concentrated on breathing and relaxing.

Over the course of the next nine and a half hours, I was led through one ridiculous question after another. Queries began with the Norfolk Southern attorney asking me any and every question he could think of. He asked me where I currently worked, what medication I was taking, where I lived, and how I felt about what had been done to me. He seemed fascinated by the idea of my nightmares.

"Is it the same nightmare? Is it a different nightmare?" he asked me, his Southern drawl evident.

"Some recurring, some different," I replied, already sick of the proceedings.

He asked me to tell him about them.

I sighed and recited, "The recurring nightmare – being forced up against the wall in the office at the diesel facility, somebody having me in a headlock, somebody feeling my genitals . . . people trying to kiss me, being pinched."

I asked him if he wanted me to go on, because I certainly could. He wanted to know when I had the nightmares, who was in them, and what each person was doing. He was relentless in his questioning.

Then, because the Norfolk Southern attorney had access to

all of my files, he questioned me about my history with the railroad. He wanted to know when I was hired, where I'd worked, and if I'd ever had problems with co-workers sexually harassing me before I came to Birmingham. It was insulting, and he treated me like I was a child. He became impatient with me when I didn't understand a question, and he hated to repeat himself. I wanted to be crystal clear on every question and refused to answer unless I understood exactly what he wanted to know.

The railroad attorney was also hostile during some lines of questioning. He wanted specifics when I told him that it seemed the entire railroad knew about my lawsuit. I told him about my friend Eddie Hickman calling and another man from Charlotte, North Carolina, that I knew. I told the man from Charlotte that I really wasn't able to talk about the suit. The railroad attorney jumped in and asked if that was the end of the conversation.

"Basically, yes, sir," I replied.

"Well, yes or no?" he countered.

"Well, yeah, we said—"

"If it wasn't, I want to know the rest of it," he interrupted. His tone was accusatory.

"We said good-bye," I finished.

Next, he delved into my mental conditions. He wanted to know everything there was to know about my anxieties, my fear of crowds, and how I had possibly been able to get married in Chattanooga. Immediately, my guard was up. It was fine if they implied whatever they wanted about me, but I was angry that they wanted to bring Marcia down to their level of questioning.

He would never have understood that getting married was something we needed to do, something that we both wanted that was outside of the horrors I was facing. He instead asked me whether or not my divorce had been final when I got married. The guy acted like I might have been a bigamist. Norfolk Southern was blindly digging in hopes they'd hit gold.

If an outsider had been listening in, it would have been difficult for him to determine exactly what the lawsuit was about based on the questions. I had to tell the lawyers the address of my house, why I renewed my South Carolina driver's license, where I attended high school, what duties I performed when I worked for my father, Marcia's life history, what brand of cigarettes I smoked, who I rented my properties to, what credit cards I used, and what jobs I applied for since being fired from the railroad. A biographer couldn't have been any more thorough.

Knowing that they were going to use all of the information they gathered to dig up dirt on me gave me an uneasy feeling deep in the pit of my stomach. The only reassuring thought I had was that I had no skeletons in my closet. I was never arrested for anything. I was never disciplined or fired on a job (besides the Norfolk Southern termination). My conscience was clear. *If they want to dig, let them dig,* I thought defiantly.

There were a lot of tricky questions asked of me. Many of them worried me, and I assumed that they'd be used against me in court. One particularly memorable question came from the railroad attorney. He asked me, "Other than DUI, have you ever been stopped or arrested?"

The question implied that I had been stopped or arrested for DUI, which I never had. That was similar to a loaded question like, "Now that you've stopped beating your wife, do y'all get along?" At least during depositions I was allowed to explain each answer, unlike during a trial where a "yes" or "no" answer was required.

There was a particularly sleazy episode towards the tail end of the deposition. Hornbuckle's lawyer had asked me all kinds of ridiculous questions, such as did I secretly enjoy his client and Thomasson harassing me. He wanted to know exactly how Thomasson had put me in a headlock. He wanted me to show someone – physically – how it was done.

The lawyer was a very large man and I didn't think that I would be able to get my arms around his shoulders, much less get him into a headlock. He asked if anyone smaller wanted to help me demonstrate. No one volunteered and Steve told me to go ahead and get the large lawyer in a headlock if that was what he wanted.

We had been in the room for over eight hours and I was a ball of nervous energy. If he wanted to see what it felt like, I saw no reason to disappoint him. The man leaned forward so that I could get my arms around his neck.

I put him in a headlock exactly the way Thomasson had locked me up – like a vise grip. I held on to the lawyer's neck with force, and I felt his neck pop two or three times. Then, I whispered in his ear, "I hope I don't break your neck."

I released him and he immediately turned everything around on me.

"Mr. court reporter, did you get that?" And to me, "What did you say? Did you say that you were going to break my neck? Did you say that?" he asked, attempting to paint me as some type of psychopath.

I told him that I hadn't said that. I told him I hoped I *didn't* break his neck. He dropped it for a couple minutes. Later, he asked if I had been teasing him when I told him that I was going to break his neck. I re-emphasized what I'd actually said. The man was impossible.

"Oh, okay. I misunderstood. I thought you were teasing me, saying you were going to break my neck. Is that the way they would do you? Would they tease you about that?" he asked.

❖   ❖

This was the first deposition in my life and I hoped it would be my last. The dirty tactics, the loaded questions, and the long hours were too much to handle. Finally, after over nine hours of questioning, Steve had enough. "We've been going more than the time allotted for it now. This deposition is over with," he said.

Afterwards, when the defendants and their attorneys had

left, Steve and Beverly apologized for the length of time. They told me that I did well and it was good that I hadn't let the lawyers rattle me.

I was informed that we finally had a court date and judge for the case. We were going to trial against a multi-billion dollar company and three of its employees on June 4, 1996. It seemed like such a long time away. I had waited for an eternity to put Norfolk Southern, Hornbuckle, Thomasson, and Summerlin in the past. The end was finally in sight and I was relieved.

Though the deposition was difficult and sleazy, it was nothing compared to the actual trial to follow.

11

HOW MANY LAWYERS DOES IT TAKE. . .

Oh, a suffering world cries for mercy
As far as the eye can see.
Lawyers around every bend in the road,
Lawyers in every tree
–Tom Paxton, "One Million Lawyers"

Birmingham, Alabama
June 3, 1996

I have held my breath as juries handed out the death penalty to innocent men, watched hundreds of legal proceedings, and cheered when justice prevailed and a good man's name was cleared – all from the comfort of my sofa. There isn't an hour that goes by on television, it seems, without a court-driven plot. I, like thousands of other viewers, was duped into believing that what I saw on television was an accurate depiction of the real thing. I was wrong.

Steve and Beverly prepared for my trial while I continued work for the auto dealership. I tried to put any thoughts of the court date out of my mind. For over a year, I wrote service reports at the dealership's maintenance shop. Through countless encounters with customers, I was no longer afraid of dealing with the public. It felt good to tell Dr. Robbins about the breakthrough. I was well on my way to recovery.

Always, though, the court date loomed in the back of my

mind. I would never be free or able to completely recover until Norfolk Southern and my attackers were a distant memory. As June 4, 1996, approached, I worked on stress-reduction exercises that Dr. Robbins taught me. I knew that I needed to remain calm, especially in a court of law.

About a week before the trial, Marcia and I traveled back down to Birmingham. The trial of Edwin Berry Martin, Jr. vs. Norfolk Southern Railway Co., Preston Lee Thomasson, Robert F. Summerlin, and Larry D. Hornbuckle was about to begin. The last time I had seen the inside of a courtroom was during my divorce. Even then, I didn't have as much riding on my shoulders as I did now. Steve and Beverly were very optimistic and defined grace under pressure. They were, after all, professionals. They knew what they had to do in order to win the case.

Choosing the jury was the first step in the trial. On June 3, 1996, my attorneys, Marcia, and I went down to the courtroom to help choose a jury of my peers. We needed jurors who would be sympathetic to my story. Those included men and women who were not supervisors or members of management at their work. We preferred self-employed jurors. Women would also make good jurors, we felt, as they were more familiar with the issue of sexual harassment.

The judge presiding over my case was the Honorable Edwin L. Nelson. In his mid-fifties and a product of the rural South, Judge Nelson was not one to mince words. When he had an opinion, he gave it. While sitting on the bench, he had at his fingertips a laptop computer. I didn't know what he could link up to with the computer, but he was constantly pounding away at the keys. I suspect that he used it to take notes on the proceedings as quickly as a court reporter.

Judge Nelson was a font of information. He cited numerous obscure court cases from the top of his head. As we gathered to begin jury deliberations, he set the tone for the rest of the trial. He outlined the way he liked things done in his courtroom. Nelson wanted a quick trial and didn't like the details of my case. He felt the case was sleazy. I couldn't tell whether he was displeased with the defendants or with me.

Before my trial began, Judge Nelson threw out the charges regarding Title VII. He decided that because I was a man and my attackers were men, there were no grounds for a claim of sexual harassment. I believed that Judge Nelson didn't want to risk making a ruling on Title VII claims, only to have it overturned on appeal. He threw out the sexual harassment charge before there was any controversy. Steve didn't allow himself time to be disappointed. For his part, he decided to try the case as he had planned all along: by informing the jurors of the atrocities I suffered at the hands of Hornbuckle, Thomasson, and Summerlin.

On my side of the courtroom sat Steve Poer, Beverly Baker, and I. On the defendant's side, there were six lawyers and my three attackers sitting at a small table. The judge asked them if they were comfortable and admitted that he couldn't think of any way to fix the problem of fitting them into the small area provided. The attorneys assured the judge that they were more than comfortable.

Representing Norfolk Southern were Crawford S. McGivaren and John Mark Graham. McGivaren was the lead council, wore expensive suits, and led the attack. He was a brilliant attorney, but too much of a cold-hearted warrior to be liked in the courtroom. He didn't seem to mind being the bad guy. He knew what he had to do to win: gloss over the facts of the case and concentrate on personally attacking me.

Michael K. Beard represented Thomasson. He was the same man who had asked me to put him in a headlock, then proceeded to manufacture threatening words from my mouth. I didn't trust Beard further than I could throw him. He attempted to paint Thomasson as an innocent victim, exploited by a disgruntled supervisor (me) to further my own agenda. He and Thomasson made a perfect pair.

Summerlin's attorney, Gayle H. Gear, was present with her client. I didn't buy into her Polyanna routine. During depositions, she had played the outsider who didn't know much. I saw her act as an attempt to "trick" me into contradicting myself. Their trouble was that I had never faltered once in all the times I had discussed the facts of my case. She could try to trick me all she wanted, and I would continue telling the truth.

Lastly, Douglas L. Key and Joseph E. Bulgarella sat next to their client, Larry Hornbuckle. Both Key and Bulgarella were unfazed by the facts of the case. Like McGivaren, they wanted to divert the jurors' attention away from the facts and onto insignificant aspects of my personal life.

At 3 P.M., eighteen potential jurors were led into the courtroom. Judge Nelson went through the procedures of jury selection.

"Good afternoon. Ladies and gentlemen, I am Judge Nelson. I will be presiding at the trial of the case for which we are about to select from among you a jury. I'll tell you a little about what the case is about and what we'll be doing, and what you may expect of us and what we expect of you."

All the jurors stood and read their names, addresses, how long they had lived there, where they were employed, where their spouses worked, and a little about their experiences in a court of law. Each side – the plaintiff's and the defendants' – was allowed four peremptory challenges. A peremptory challenge of a juror could be about anything. If Steve didn't like the way a juror parted his hair or the way she applied makeup, he could get rid of her. It didn't matter. After the four peremptory challenges, the only way a juror could be eliminated was with a challenge for cause. A challenge for cause was imposed if the juror had a conflict of interest in the case. For example, if potential juror number twelve had a spouse who worked in Norfolk Southern management, that would represent a definite conflict of interest.

After each side had used up its strikes, we would be left with the jury. That meant that we would have a jury of ten if we each used all four strikes and there were no challenges for cause. I didn't care how many jurors we had, as long as they were honest and looked at the facts of the case before making their judgement. Before any juror was dismissed, the lawyers were allowed to ask questions of them.

Steve began with voir dire ("to speak the truth"), a mini-hearing to decide which jurors each side wanted. During voir dire, each attorney asks questions to determine whether a potential juror would be hostile or friendly to each respective side. Steve asked if any of the jurors knew anyone in the courtroom, whether or not they had ever filed suit against anyone, and if they were ever harassed in any way on the job. We wanted jurors that could relate to my case.

My attackers' attorneys asked questions of the jurors about their backgrounds and views on supervisory positions, medical knowledge, and acceptance of foul language. From their questions, I could tell that it was going to be a witch-hunt of a trial. The opposition's attorneys weren't going to be playing fair. Steve and Beverly had warned me before, but I was finally getting my first taste of the real thing.

Judge Nelson had restricted the voir dire to twenty-five minutes per side. After both sides were finished, it was time to decide on the jury. First, McGivaren asked for a side panel, away from the ears of the potential jurors. He submitted a challenge for cause against one juror who had a pending harassment claim. Steve fought to keep her on, but in the end Judge Nelson struck her from the group.

We took a fifteen-minute recess while we debated which jurors to keep and which to strike. Towards the end, we had to make a decision between two jurors, and Steve asked me which one I wanted to keep. I was floored. I told him to go ahead and flip a coin to decide. He told me that this was a very important decision and couldn't be decided so haphazardly. In the end, I let him decide.

We went back into the courtroom to begin our peremptory challenges, but Beard had other plans. As soon as we got back into the courtroom, he asked for another private meeting with Judge Nelson. If I thought that his tactics during my deposition were underhanded, he was about to one-up himself. He told the judge that Thomasson had observed Marcia talking with a potential juror's husband and taking notes. These were serious allegations of jury tampering. I knew that Marcia would never do anything to jeopardize my case.

The judge called the juror back and questioned her. When asked if Marcia had approached her through her husband, she flatly denied it. She told Judge Nelson that her husband had approached her about a comment she had made during questioning. It involved her husband being on disability and he wanted to make sure she related the fact that he wasn't injured on the job, but was on disability because of a weak heart. There was no coercion by Marcia and the judge was satisfied.

At 5 P.M. we selected a jury. Each side struck four jurors and we were left with nine people. The others were asked to leave the courtroom. I looked out over the faces of the nine jurors and wondered what their decision would be at trial's end. There was no way to tell. I felt the acid churning in my stomach.

Just when I thought we were done for the day, Beard again accused my wife of having conversation with the juror's husband. Steve stood up and told the court that it was the husband that was talking to Marcia, not the other way around. He had instructed Marcia not to talk with him, but he kept approaching her. The judge told Steve to ask Marcia to move away from him. When there were no more questions or comments asked, Judge Nelson ended the proceedings.

"All right," he said. "Thank you very much. See you promptly at nine o'clock tomorrow morning." My trial was about to begin.

❖   ❖

That night I didn't sleep well. I tossed and turned in the motel bed. Marcia and I watched television to try and keep our minds off the trial, but it was no use. It was very late before I got to sleep, and a couple hours later I was getting dressed for court. After I adjusted my tie in the foggy bathroom mirror, Marcia and I left for the courthouse. It was going to be a long week.

Judge Nelson began the trial by having the jury sworn in. He gave them some preliminary instructions. "Your duty or your job is to decide questions of fact and to decide what the facts are. I decide questions of law and procedure. Then when you have heard all of the evidence, during your deliberations, you will decide the facts and apply to those facts the law which I will tell you about in some detail."

He then outlined the entire case for the jury, taking special care to discuss FELA and EEOC claims. Finally, it was time for opening statements.

Steve stood before the jury and began speaking. He was cordial and polite. He introduced himself again and told the jury that he and Beverly had been involved with my case for almost two years. He told them that three men who did not want me there had ganged up on me, and Norfolk Southern did not provide me with a safe workplace. Steve had a way of putting things into perspective.

"Sometimes I like to say, folks, what you have heard is basically a puzzle, each of the witnesses being a piece of the puzzle. You don't see the puzzle all at one time. You see it one piece at a time. And basically, when we're through putting our puzzle together, we hope that you see the picture we intend for you to see based on the facts and the witnesses and the exhibits."

He gave the jury my background. It was strange finding myself in a room where a man poured out pieces of my life to complete strangers so that they could get to know me. Steve told them about my education, where I had worked before the railroad, and how I began my career with Norfolk Southern. He built up my story piece by piece. The jurors listened as he told them how I was a responsible and dedicated employee for over fifteen years. When he got to the first words Hornbuckle greeted me with, you could see the shock in the jurors' eyes. They were on the edge of their seats when he delved into all of the details of my case.

"[Mr. Martin] has got some friends at the railroad that are going to come down here and tell you what a good worker he was, what a good supervisor he was before coming to Birmingham, because [the defendants] are now attacking him as incompetent and unable to do the job," said Steve. He told them about the testimony we would be presenting and thanked them for their time.

Crawford McGivaren was up next. His opening statement was full of accusations and colorful statements. One of his first was "I don't suppose it will come as any surprise to you that even the thinnest pancakes have got two sides." He said of me that "the job was running him, he wasn't running the job." McGivaren tried to paint a picture of me as a wholly incompetent worker.

He implied to the jury that I was more interested in returning to South Carolina to work on my house than I was in doing my job correctly. He told them that I was prone to exaggeration, I had the power to stop the actions at any time, and that Norfolk Southern had provided me with ample training and venues to fix the problem myself. Furthermore, he told them that the behavior of the individual defendants was not nearly as frequent as I would have them believe. McGivaren had effectively distanced Norfolk Southern from Hornbuckle, Thomasson, and Summerlin.

Beard began by telling the jury what a stand-up guy Thomasson was. Apparently, he and Thomasson had attended the same high school.

"You're going to hear and the evidence in this case will be this: that what Mr. Thomasson did was horseplay," Beard told the jury. He admitted that his client pinched people or "goosed" them on the back of the leg, just as he did with his children. His client would never intentionally harm anyone, much less put someone in a headlock. He also admitted that Thomasson made kissing sounds to fellow employees. Beard emphasized that his client always stopped when asked to.

As for me and my claims, Beard told the jury that it was nonsense. After all, I was Thomasson's supervisor and had the power to stop Thomasson's behavior any time I wanted to. He told the jury that I would laugh when I told Thomasson to stop and that I didn't seem to mind the attention. I saw red. Beard was antagonizing me on a personal level, and I found it fitting that he should be representing Thomasson.

"Now I'm not going to tell you much about the medical part of this," he told the jury, "because all it is is you go to a psychologist or you go to a counselor and you recite these God awful things that you say happened to you, and they listen to them and they say, 'Gee, this person is anxious,' and they give him some kind of medication."

I wondered what the mental health community would say about his estimation of their work. Clearly, Beard was a man not concerned with being liked. I had seen him only three times and already I despised him.

During jury deliberations, Gear made several references to how nervous she was. It showed in her opening statements. She really laid it on thick for the jury. She made Summerlin seem like a war hero who deserved the Medal of Honor.

"Through his own testimony, I think you'll see he's very proud of serving his country," said Gear. "He does not see it in any way as having negative impact on his overall life, except to make him far more considerate and far more responsible to his company and to his family." The way her statement was worded, she made it seem to the jury that I was of the opinion that his military service was a negative factor.

Gear talked to the jury about each of the times I had told my story. First I told it to my attorneys. Then I told it to the EEOC. Then I told my doctors. Then I related it during the railroad investigation. Finally, she told them I would be telling my story again to them.

"I think the potential is there for an embellishment and exaggeration, but thankfully we have juries to sort those kinds of things out, and we will provide testimony in the sorting." What she failed to mention is that my story never once changed. From the first time I told Marcia my story to the nine-and-a-half hour deposition, I never faltered. It was burned into my brain. I couldn't forget the horrors committed against me if I lived to be a hundred and fifty years old.

Last up was Bulgarella. Because Hornbuckle was named last on the complaint, Bulgarella would always go last in order. He misled the jury almost from the beginning.

"I want to make this as clear as I can, that Mr. Hornbuckle did absolutely nothing that would injure Mr. Martin," he said. He admitted that his client had asked to see my "dick," but that I took the joke out of context. He explained with a few words exactly how the trial was going to be fought by him and the other defendants' attorneys: by attacking me.

"One of the things you're going to ask yourself is why would Mr. Martin create these things?" he informed the jury. "You're going to hear evidence about Mr. Martin's character. You're going to hear evidence about the possible motives. You're going to hear evidence about his lack of competence on the job. And when you hear this evidence, ask yourself if those possibly can't be the answers as to why he would make these allegations."

I had no physical evidence. I had very few corroborating witnesses, and none that had observed the worst. The entire railroad was against me. I had only my good name and my honesty. I realized then that the entire case would come down to one thing: their word against mine.

12

TAKING THE STAND

Victory at all costs, victory in spite of all terror,
victory however long and hard the road may be,
for without victory there is no survival.
–Winston Churchill, May 13, 1940

Birmingham, Alabama
June 4, 1996

My trial began on June 4, 1996, with Steve Poer putting me on the stand. I was sworn in and took a seat. I was extremely nervous, but knew that Steve would guide me through my testimony. It wasn't Steve that I was worried about, though. The mere thought of McGivaren or Beard standing before me and misrepresenting the facts gave me anxiety. I pushed those thoughts from my mind and concentrated on Steve's voice.

Steve led me through a brief background of my work history and family. He asked me about my family's involvement with the locomotive industry, about my children, and my home. I felt comfortable with his line of questioning. He began slowly, but eventually found his way to the important facts of the case. He didn't beat around the bush.

"Let me ask you, Mr. Martin, right up front, are you homosexual?" he asked.

"No, sir," I replied.

It didn't matter that Judge Nelson had thrown out the sexual harassment charges. We were going to try the case as if he hadn't. There was no way the jury wasn't going to receive as much of the information as we could get across. It was impossible to give the jury your entire story. There were certain ways that we had to present the evidence. Steve's approach was logical and designed to make certain key points stick in the jury's mind. He planted seeds that later would grow and be harvested.

When Steve and Beverly interviewed me before the trial, I didn't know which parts of what I told them would be included in my testimony. Before the trial, as we went over my testimony, I was impressed with the way they had pieced together all of the little pieces of data to form the story of my life. I never thought about my interview with the railroad in 1979 and beating out a hundred applicants for the job. I didn't think about being promoted to a foreman only three years later. My testimony made me feel better about myself. It was like Steve had asked me to list my accomplishments in order and then acknowledge them in front of a room full of people.

Steve had a knack for nipping things in the bud. He had a quick mind and counterattacked before the opposition knew what he was doing. He took Beard's statement about "horseplay" and went with it.

"Did you play sports while you were in high school?" asked Steve.

"Yes, sir, I did."

"And were you exposed to locker room humor, that type of thing, horseplay, whatever, in the locker rooms as an athlete?"

"Yes, sir, I was," I told him.

"And were you ever particularly or overly offended by any of that conduct, sir?" he asked.

I told him that I wasn't, and we immediately went on to the subject of my transfer to Birmingham. Steve had effectively told the jury that if all I was exposed to in Birmingham was horseplay, I wouldn't have been offended. He didn't need to ask me if I thought that Hornbuckle and Thomasson were engaged in good-natured horseplay.

One of my charges against the railroad was compensation for lost future wages. This was pivotal to any settlement I might receive. We wanted the jury to know that if I had stayed with Norfolk Southern, I would have earned quite a bit more money than I was currently making as a service writer with the auto dealership. McGivaren had a fit with my testimony about lost benefits and future lost wages.

Steve asked me to discuss my 401(k) plan, medical benefits, and the amount of money I would have earned had I retired from the railroad at age 65. McGivaren objected to every question, only to have his objections overruled by Judge Nelson.

McGivaren's objections stemmed from his opinion that I was not "expert" enough to determine my lost wages. He implied that I was not capable of figuring out the interest rates, loss of benefits, or my investments. Steve countered cleverly.

"Mr. Martin, can you read?" he asked. I answered "yes."

"Do you have occasion to read the newspapers and such?" Again, I answered "yes."

Steve's questions showed the jury that not only was anybody capable of determining their own financial status, but that McGivaren's objections were insulting to me and any "normal" person, including members of the jury. McGivaren argued and delayed proceedings with objections about my qualifications. Steve neatly sorted through the objections and proceeded after the judge overruled each of McGivaren's protests.

For the next few hours, Steve led me through the details of my harassment at Birmingham. There were very few interruptions, which was fine by me. It was difficult enough to tell a room of complete strangers about the intimate details of my harassment. Slowly, but surely, we waded through the muck of what had been done to me by Hornbuckle, Thomasson, and Summerlin. Around 4 P.M. we finished with lost future wages and my job at the automotive dealership. I felt drained, but knew I was in for a real attack the next morning.

I slept poorly and made it to the courtroom about an hour early. At 9 A.M. on June 5, the cross-examinations began.

McGivaren got first crack at me. To say that he was hostile was an understatement. I never expected it to be easy, but he was making it very difficult to keep my mind on the facts at hand. I suppose that his objective was to confuse me.

McGivaren asked me about notes I had made on the incidents at the railroad. One of the entries was dated November 19, 1993, and he was attempting to make it look like I had kept a running diary of all that had happened. I tried explaining that most of the notes I made were done after the fact, but McGivaren pretended not to listen. He asked how I could have made the November 19th notation afterwards if the date was written right next to the note. He played dumb when I told him that I wrote the date down (as I remembered it) some four months later.

McGivaren also didn't present my complete notes into evidence. Instead, he took out two pages from several I had turned over. He asked me specific questions only about those two pages, disregarding the complete package.

I had a feeling that my marriage to Marcia would eventually come under fire, and I wasn't disappointed. McGivaren wondered how I could possibly get married in the midst of such a horrible existence. He asked me about my mental faculties at the time and any physical handicaps that had resulted from the harassment.

"So immediately following the night that you spent probably the most fearsome night in your life, you and your girlfriend went and got married?" he asked, the sarcasm evident in his voice.

I found it difficult, through my anger, to tell him that we had gotten married despite all that was happening. We got married and forgot my problems for a brief moment. Instead, I answered that "yes," we had gotten married shortly after I spent the night hiding on a locomotive.

Then McGivaren tried to paint my subsequent two-week

medical leave as nothing more than a honeymoon at the railroad's expense. He made it seem like Marcia and I had escaped to Panama City Beach and spent the week frolicking in the surf and sun. I told him that the place we stayed was not near the beach. Answering another question, I told McGivaren and the jury that Marcia and I could not consummate our marriage at that time.

We broke for lunch and Steve told me I was doing just fine. He told me not to let them rattle me up there on the stand. I told him it was easier said than done. After lunch, it was Beard's turn for examination. I tried to prepare myself for any tricky tactics he might attempt.

Beard went off on various tangents to divert the jury's mind from the facts. He didn't want to delve into the deviant behavior and sexual harassment I was subjected to at the hands of his client and his client's friends. He asked me instead about an inspection I had made on a locomotive's flange, the rim of the engine's wheels that kept the train on the tracks. The incident in question went back to January of 1989, some four and a half years before I came to Birmingham. He attempted to portray me as a problem employee who didn't know what he was doing. Unfortunately for him, I had not been disciplined for the incident. I had been warned by my supervisor at the time to watch out for thin flanges. That was the only "dirt" that Beard could find in my railroad file, so he searched elsewhere.

During the learning phase of my time at Birmingham, my subordinates and I once had gotten our signals crossed. The blue flag warning system was taken down prematurely and a train was moved before it was ready. In the process, some fuel hoses were pulled loose from the fuel tanks.

Beard jumped at the supposed incompetence I had shown. It didn't matter that incidents like that were common on the railroad. He pretended that I had caused a disaster on par with the Hindenberg explosion. In fact, incidents like the one in question were common enough to warrant having many extra fuel hoses in the supply shack.

Beard was downright hostile towards me. Steve objected a few times to comments made by the sarcastic attorney. At one point during questioning, Beard said, "Is there any reason that you couldn't say 'yes, sir' or 'no, sir' to that question? I mean, it seems to me it either was or wasn't. I don't understand this 'could be' stuff."

Before Steve could object, Beard was off on another tangent. His questions were so inflammatory that at one point he had to apologize to the judge and to me in order to save face.

Beard brought up Bishop's offer to me for a transfer. I told the court that Bishop had offered to transfer and promote me shortly after I had filed charges against the railroad. I hadn't commented to Bishop on his offer. Beard questioned me with his usual antagonism.

"And if you had taken him up on what you say was Mr. Bishop's word, you wouldn't be here asking eight [sic] people to give you $17,000 a year out of Mr. Thomasson's pocket, would you?" He had taken my difference in pay figure and misrepresented my testimony. Steve immediately objected.

Amazingly, the judge overruled the objection. I explained that I never considered Bishop's offer of transfer as legitimate since he hadn't given it to me in writing. Beard thanked the jury and sat down.

Gayle Gear stepped up and concentrated on outside events. She asked me what kind of vehicle I owned when I came to Birmingham. She asked what I had brought with me when I moved. Even my Alabama driver's license test came under question. Her nervousness showed as she questioned me about my pending divorce when I moved to Alabama. I explained to her over and over again that I was not emotionally upset over the divorce. She didn't understand that the relationship had gradually come to an end and didn't cause me any undue stress.

She questioned me about which words in the English language I found offensive. She asked me about "cunt," "pussy," and "dick." She then implied that I had used those words at the yard. I told her that I had never used those words and that I found them offensive. She didn't take into account the context in which the defendants used the words.

Finally, we reached the point where Steve could re-direct questions to me. He brought up the notes that McGivaren had taken out of context. He asked me if the notes presented and discussed by McGivaren were my complete notes. Sensing a side issue, Judge Nelson excused the jury for a break, and we got into a big discussion about my notes. The defense claimed that Steve and Beverly did not offer up the notes. Steve said he had proof that they were offered. McGivaren contended that Steve attempted to hide the notes from defense counsel. The fight got dirty and the judge made personal observations about where we were headed.

"Now you're putting me in the position where I have got to make credibility choices between lawyers. I would rather not do that. You make me do it, and I will do it, and I will call one of you untruthful. That's not something I would prefer to do," he told McGivaren and Steve. He waived judgment on the notes until the next morning.

For the next hour, until late afternoon, McGivaren and Beard questioned me again.

During the formal investigations into the defendants, I had been disappointed that none of my subordinates spoke up about what they had witnessed. I understood their reasoning, though. They were afraid of losing their jobs. At the time of the trial, I got lucky. Curtis Brierly, a former subordinate, was no longer an employee of Norfolk Southern, and he agreed to serve as my witness. I was happy to finally have someone stand up for the truth.

Brierly was a good witness and didn't appear nervous. He answered honestly. Steve didn't know what Brierly had witnessed, so he asked him many questions to determine the extent of his knowledge. Brierly was not the smoking gun, and we didn't expect he would be. We hoped that he could at least verify some of the events that happened at the diesel shop, and he did.

After many questions, Brierly admitted to seeing Hornbuckle and Thomasson physically "messing" with me. He had heard Hornbuckle laughing about inferring that I would be losing my job shortly and telling me not to bother buying a house. Also, Brierly verified numerous remarks made by Hornbuckle, including "AIDS 3" and "Three Muske-Queers."

Steve asked Brierly if Stutsman and Bishop had interviewed him after I had brought charges. He said he had.

"And did you tell them everything that you had seen and observed out there at the railroad?" asked Steve.

"No," answered Brierly.

"Why not?"

"I didn't know how it would affect my job," Brierly told the jury.

Beard cross-examined Brierly first, and threw some of the usual tricky questions at the witness. He asked Brierly if he had been honest in his assessment of my job performance. He said he had.

"And did you not say at that time that Mr. Martin had a habit of violating the blue flag rule?" asked Beard.

"I didn't say he had a habit of violating the blue flag rule. I know he violated it one time," corrected Brierly.

I tried to keep my composure as Beard attempted to destroy my character with underhanded tactics and false accusations. I felt like jumping up half a dozen times to clarify points that McGivaren and Beard were trying to make. It was extremely difficult to answer only "yes" or "no" to questions that required explanations. If a witness attempted to explain his answer, the judge would cut him off or the opposing attorney would object.

The defendants made a big deal of the fact that I didn't go to Norfolk Southern's Equal Employment Opportunity (EEO) office before filing my court case. They saw this "breach" as proof positive that I did not follow the correct chain of command. Apparently there was a large poster describing the railroad's EEO policy hanging in the back of the office near the parking lot. Norfolk Southern contended that the poster was easily accessible and in plain view of all employees.

During my deposition and pre-trial questioning, I said that I had never seen any such poster. Therefore, I went first to an attorney, then to the federal EEOC. Brierly admitted that he had never seen or heard of the poster, either.

After Brierly finished, Judge Nelson called it a day. He made a reference to taking a bath with strong soap that night. I felt good and was thankful that Brierly had agreed to serve as my witness. He was the only co-worker from Birmingham to testify for me. Apparently, Hornbuckle and Thomasson had many that were going to serve as character witnesses. I wanted to be finished with the entire trial and go home to South Carolina.

❖   ❖

The next day, June 6, 1996, Steve had many witnesses to call. Judge Nelson wanted to get the trial over with. According to him, we were already running behind. Steve told him that he would try to streamline the day's testimony as much as possible.

"You ever hear the story about Judge Lynne sentencing the old man to forty-five years in prison?" asked Judge Nelson of Steve. "He said, 'Judge, I don't think I can handle that.' And he said, 'Do the best you can.'"

"I understand," answered Steve.

Beverly Baker handled questions for our next witness – my sister, Lynn Dodds. Because she is a bookkeeper for several companies, she became our "expert" witness regarding finances. Beverly had her go through her educational and vocational background. Lynn told the jury that she took care of my rental properties for me while I was out of town and testified that she had prepared my taxes.

Beverly asked her questions about my loss of income.

Lynn told the court that she took over the construction of my house. It had been a big deal to McGivaren that I was still building a house in South Carolina while working in Birmingham. He saw a conspiracy in my actions, and he attempted to make it seem like I had planned on suing the railroad all along in order to move back home and finish work on my house. Lynn made that notion seem ridiculous.

Lynn was an excellent source for verifying my mental state during the time of my harassment. I had talked to her several times on the telephone. She also described my weight loss that she and my mother had noticed during Christmas. At one point, she broke down crying on the stand. She had been horrified by what I went through and it showed in her testimony.

When Beard cross-examined her, he concentrated on my rental properties. I couldn't see what any questions about rental properties had to do with Thomasson putting me in a headlock and grabbing my genitals. Beard tried to make me out as a wealthy landlord, but Lynn told him that I didn't own any of the properties outright. She told him that I still paid a mortgage on all of them. Besides, she informed the jury, I sold three of the five properties after losing my job with the railroad because I couldn't afford to keep them.

Next, Steve questioned Eddie Hickman, my friend who worked for Norfolk Southern. Eddie took a big risk testifying for me, and I knew that life would not be easy for him after doing so. He verified that word had spread as far away as South Carolina about my lawsuit. He told the jury about the rumors he had heard about my sexuality and being a troublemaker. In his opinion, there was no way that I could continue to work for the railroad.

Eddie also cleared up the "thin flange" testimony. The defense tried to show me as a lax employee who had almost derailed a train. Eddie explained that a thin flange was not enough to derail a train. He also explained that the flange could have worn down between the time I inspected it in Spartanburg, South Carolina, and the time it reached Columbia, South Carolina, a distance of over 100 miles.

Marcia was put on the stand after Eddie. I was most worried about her testifying. I knew it wouldn't be easy because she was more involved than any of the others. Her testimony was very emotional and, bless her heart, she answered every question, no matter how personal.

McGivaren and Beard attempted to tear apart our relationship and make it seem dirty. She stood up to them and told them that, while our relationship began as a friendship, the romance wasn't far behind. A couple times, when she found herself defending our actions together (getting married, going to a restaurant) she broke down in tears. But she eventually got through the testimony.

When she was finished, we took a lunch break. I hugged her tightly and told her that she had done well. Marcia felt like she might have hurt my case with her testimony, but I explained that the defense was fishing for anything they could find. I told her that the jury knew what the case was really about. I only wished that I could believe that.

After lunch we began medical testimony. Because we couldn't ask all of my medical doctors and counselors to wait around in court to testify, we made videotaped depositions. Present during videotaping was a court-appointed stenographer. All witnesses were sworn in. The videotapes carried the same weight as personal testimony would.

Judge Nelson didn't want Steve to play all of the testimony because of length. Steve promised to only play the parts he felt were important. Judge Nelson was still apprehensive. In the end, Steve agreed to play a short clip from each and then read excerpts from the transcripts. During reading, Steve would play the part of himself, and Beverly would sit on the stand and play the part of each doctor.

The jury found it boring. At one point a juror asked if he could take a nap. Judge Nelson said he'd wake anyone if he saw they were sleeping. Steve assured the jurors that he'd turn up the volume. There was much testimony regarding my symptoms and treatment. Dr. Robbins was by far the most helpful witness because I had seen her more than thirty-five times.

The defense tried to discredit the counselors because they were not officially "psychologists." Both were licensed therapists, though, and Robbins had a doctorate in counseling. There was no surprise in any of the testimony, and Steve managed to wrap it up fairly quickly the next day.

After medical testimonies, Steve's case rested. Our part in presenting the case was over. I prayed that the jury had heard enough to form an opinion. Directly after we declare the case rested, the defense attorneys presented Judge Nelson with matter-of-law motions. Basically, matter-of-law motions ask for judgment based on the testimony already heard. Because we were finished with my case, the defense counselors asked for summary judgment on the trial up to that point.

Gear made a motion stating that the evidence presented did not implicate her client, Summerlin. Steve conceded that the case against Summerlin was our weakest. Consequently, Judge Nelson threw out the case against Summerlin and he was excused.

Judge Nelson also threw out the "tort of outrage" claims against Hornbuckle and Thomasson. The particulars of the charge were difficult to prove, and we hadn't proven that I was subjected to cruel and unusual emotional duress. Hornbuckle and Thomasson still faced charges of assault and battery and invasion of privacy.

All charges stood against Norfolk Southern, something that would cause McGivaren to protect his company with every half-truth and false allegation he could get his hands on.

13

THE BOYS' CLUB

The character attack began the very day Steve and Beverly finished presenting my case. It hardly mattered that Hornbuckle and Thomasson were sworn in when they testified. They were immoral men who did not care about truth. The same could be said for their witnesses. Most of the testimony given had absolutely nothing to do with the lawsuit. There was testimony given designed solely to ruin my name and the fifteen years of hard work I had given the railroad.

"The truth, the whole truth, and nothing but the truth" seemed an option to the defense, an oath taken out of tradition. They might as well have sworn on a dictionary for all the truth that came out of their mouths.

My old boss, Gerald Benson, took the stand first. As the first-shift general foreman, Benson was, according to McGivaren, in the unique position to tell the court how incompetent I was. McGivaren began the questions slowly and deliberately. He asked Benson if he remembered my first weeks at the Norris diesel shop in Birmingham. Benson told the court that I couldn't seem to grasp the work. He felt that, despite my training, I wasn't a competent enough employee to handle the busy job.

In any locomotive facility across the nation, a team of men services each train. A locomotive shop is only as good as the team of men who work there. Because Benson worked first shift – and never ventured into third-shift territory – he was not in a position to tell the court that I was incompetent. He didn't know about my subordinates sleeping on the job. He didn't know how the third-shift team worked together.

What he did know was that I had expressed to him difficulty with Hornbuckle, Thomasson, and Summerlin. Conveniently, though, he forgot all about my talks with him about the lack of cooperation from Hornbuckle. Benson lied on the stand. He told the court flatly that he did not talk to me about my problems.

"Mr. Benson, did Mr. Martin at any time, from November of 1993 until April of 1994, ever come to you and complain to you about his relationship with any of the people he was working with on the third shift?" asked McGivaren.

"No," answered Benson.

When Beard questioned Benson, he employed all of his best character assassination techniques by ignoring the subject of the lawsuit. He asked Benson about my pulling down fuel hoses, about wheel flange measurements, and whether I had the power to fire Thomasson or send him home for ten days as a reprimand.

Benson played dumb the entire time Beard questioned him. He knew all of the rules backwards and forwards, and he had never witnessed anything out of the ordinary with anyone but me. It was ridiculous. The only thing he admitted was that I had "jokingly" told him that the men on third shift were "crazy."

Joseph Bulgarella, Hornbuckle's attorney, was next in line. Bulgarella asked Benson to clarify the chain of command. He asked him if I had ever told him about Hornbuckle specifically. Benson said I hadn't. As far as Benson was concerned, I had never told anyone about problems during third shift.

When it was time for cross-examination, Steve was ready. He questioned Benson on his current job and station. Steve and I both knew that Benson had been disciplined and demoted by Norfolk Southern for his part in ignoring my complaints. The trouble was, Benson didn't seem to know.

"I take it you moved to Norfolk, Virginia, on your own, is that right?" asked Steve.

"I was transferred there by the company," said Benson.

"Why was it that you were transferred to Norfolk, Virginia, after spending your entire career with the railroad, sir?"

"Well, sir, to be perfectly honest, I do not know," answered Benson.

Steve asked him if his current job was a lower ranking one than his previous as a general foreman. Benson agreed that it was. He also agreed that he was paid less since his demotion and transfer.

"So am I correct in assuming that you were demoted a level, you got a cut in pay, and you got sent to Norfolk, Virginia, after having spent your entire career in Birmingham, Alabama, and all of this was done and you have no idea why it happened to you?" asked an astounded Steve.

Benson was obstinate on the stand. Steve couldn't believe that Benson had no idea why he had been demoted. Benson claimed that he had been asking around for the past two years, but to no avail. He claimed that various supervisors were "still checking" into the situation for him.

"Still checking. Isn't it true that you were disciplined for your involvement in this?" asked Steve, his voice rising.

"I suppose one could assume that," admitted Benson.

Steve went on to question Benson about the language on the railroad. Benson admitted that it was wholly inappropriate. He told the court that he heard Hornbuckle use the phrase "can I see your dick?" on numerous occasions but had done nothing to put a stop to it. Steve asked him why. Benson told him that doctors had asked him that same question. Steve immediately got Benson to acknowledge that Hornbuckle was not a doctor and that his using the phrase was indeed inappropriate behavior.

Steve knew his business and how to take apart a witness's rehearsed testimony. He led into it slowly. First, he asked how long Benson had been down in Birmingham before the trial. He told him three days. Next, he asked if he had met with the railroad attorneys since he had been down. Benson told the court that he'd met with them twice. Last, Steve asked Benson if he had gone over the testimony he had given today.

At this point, McGivaren jumped up and objected. Judge Nelson overruled and allowed Steve to go on. McGivaren wasn't about to give up, though. After McGivaren argued with the judge again, the witness was instructed to answer the question. Benson replied with a quiet, "he was just telling me to tell the truth and stay calm."

Steve had effectively cast doubt in the jurors' eyes as to the credibility of Benson. Later, when Benson told the court that I was not competent at my job, it didn't have as much merit. He admitted leaving me alone while he went to lunch. Steve asked him why he would leave an "incompetent" man alone with a job that he wasn't qualified to do. Benson said that it was always done. With that, we were finished for the weekend. We left the courtroom to a rainy world.

❖   ❖

Marcia and I were in desperate need of a relaxing weekend. I looked forward to swimming in the hotel pool and generally kicking back. I didn't want to think about the witnesses the defense would put on the stand Monday. I knew that they wouldn't be kind in their assessment of my job performance.

Steve, Beverly, Marcia, and I went to dinner over the weekend. I asked Steve what the heck was going on that they were attacking me this way. He told me that this was how lawsuits of this type were always fought. If the defense team could turn the focus away from the facts of the case, they had a better chance of getting a judgment in their favor. It was like hunting ducks: you set out your decoys and blasted the ducks out of the sky when they least expected it. The good news was that decoys did not fool Steve and Beverly; their focus on the end result was absolute.

On Monday, the defense had eight witnesses on the stand, all of them with one purpose in mind: to ruin my credibility. It was inexplicable to me that so many people seemed out to get me. However, when there was a potential payoff by a large company at stake, that company would do everything in its power to get off scot-free. That day was going to be an uphill battle for my attorneys and me.

McGivaren first called Bennett, the master mechanic in Birmingham when I arrived to the job, to the stand. The three defense attorneys questioned him briefly. Bennet told the court that he had met me on only two occasions, when I first arrived and when I requested vacation time for Christmas.

On no occasion, he testified, had I told him about troubles I was having. At no time did he indicate to me that he thought Hornbuckle was "strange." I still remembered my orientation with Bennett when he waved his hand from side to side and told me that Hornbuckle was strange. I still remembered the car men laughing when they heard I was going to be working with Hornbuckle. Conveniently, Bennett didn't remember any of those conversations.

Instead, all that he remembered was hearing from Benson that I was not doing my job very well. Bennett told the court about his "open door" policy with all of his employees and said that I could have come to him at any time. He never had any problems with Hornbuckle, nor had he ever had to discipline him. He told the court that my job in South Carolina was much easier than my job in Alabama due to the number of trains that passed through each facility. In South Carolina, only ten to fifteen trains passed through each day. In Alabama, between sixty and seventy-five trains came through.

Steve cross-examined and asked Bennett how he could possibly have had an open-door policy when he had thirteen facilities to manage in over three states. Steve made it clear to the jury that it was highly unlikely that Bennett was as available to his more than 250 employees as he would have everyone believe. Bennett also admitted that he may have called Hornbuckle strange, especially after Steve pointed out that Bishop (Bennett's replacement) had heard the same thing from Bennett.

Bennett also told the jury that I might have been fired had I physically assaulted Thomasson or Hornbuckle. The last thing Steve asked Bennett was about the procedure for reporting a problem and whether it was included in any rules books. Bennett admitted, for the record, that it was not written down anywhere as far as he knew.

Next on the stand was Mark Bishop, the mechanical supervisor for Alabama after Bennett was transferred. Bishop was responsible for the initial investigations into my charges, along with Stutsman, that resulted in the firings of Hornbuckle, Thomasson, and Summerlin.

Immediately things went wrong when Bishop turned what happened around. He told the court that I was the one who had asked for a transfer and promotion, not the other way around. He said that he didn't have the authority to grant me these requests. He also said that I was the one who asked for police protection. I kept my cool as best I could amidst his lies.

Bishop was not the same man who had conducted the investigations into Hornbuckle and friends. Where he was "on my side" before, now he seemed only to find fault in my actions, job, and accounts of the harassment. He had definitely changed sides. His answers were so obviously rehearsed that I thought I was watching a play. He contradicted points in the investigation that he himself had proven. Bishop was bending over backwards to help the defense. He had probably been pressured by the railroad to do so. After all, he still had to work there.

When Steve questioned Bishop, he asked him if he had ever witnessed any of the activities on the third shift. He said he had not. Steve asked Bishop if an employee had opened his locked office on the night the EEOC charge arrived at the railroad. He said one had. Bishop also verified that the employee had called Hornbuckle and told him of my EEOC charges.

Then, Steve attempted to question Bishop about the union's Public Law Board that later re-instated Hornbuckle, Thomasson, and Summerlin to their jobs at the railroad. Bishop had been a witness at these hearings and had volunteered information. For example, during Hornbuckle's hearing, Bishop stated that there was no question in his mind that the charges were appropriate.

McGivaren had a fit when Steve tried to question Bishop on those hearings. The judge asked to see the attorneys out in his chambers, and he eventually ruled in favor of McGivaren. Furthermore, he told Steve, "Let's try to finish this trial, please. Let's go."

Despite the judge not allowing Steve to fully cross-examine the witness, the jury heard what Steve had wanted them to hear. Bishop had, at one point, believed that the charges I filed against Hornbuckle and his buddies were accurate. It didn't matter that he was being a difficult witness on the stand now. Steve finished with Bishop and we went on to the next witness for the defense.

There were two more minor witnesses for the defense before we went to lunch. Both men had been employed by the railroad during the same time I was in Birmingham. Neither man worked with me during the third shift, so neither was in a position to offer any useful testimony. Both claimed that I was not competent at my job. The defense attorneys were flooding the courtroom with so-called witnesses to defame my character. I hoped the jury wasn't buying into their sleazy tactics.

After lunch, McGivaren rested the case for the railroad. The ball was now in Beard's court as he called his client to the

stand. Thomasson was sworn in and Beard began his questions. He asked him all about his wife and children. I thought
I was going to need boots to wade through the muck. If Beard
had nominated Thomasson for the "Father of the Year" award,
I wouldn't have been surprised.

"Do you do any work with the Boy Scouts?" asked Beard,
suddenly full of compassion.

"Yes, sir. I'm an active volunteer with the Boy Scouts,"
beamed Thomasson.

As Thomasson told the court about his volunteer responsibilities with the Boy Scouts, he didn't sound any different from
any other father who was involved with his son's scouting. But
Beard laid it on thickly. Thomasson let it be known to the jury
that he was also involved in a youth football league. Sadly, the
witness said, because of the charges I had brought about, he
was not allowed to volunteer with the Boy Scouts any longer.
Fortunately, though, the football league knew what a good man
he was and allowed him to stay on.

I couldn't believe the gall of the man. He and Beard were
blaming all of his current troubles on me. Thomasson told the
room that he had no idea why I would bring about these false
charges on him. After repeatedly putting me in headlocks, attempting to kiss me, and pinching me on the rear, Thomasson
was telling the jury that he was just another average father
who loved his wife and children. I couldn't help but think that
even Genghis Khan had a mother who loved him.

As for Thomasson making "kissy" faces at me, he said that I
had it all wrong. There was a saying attached to the puckering
of the lips. Whenever he did that, he would say, "Who loves
you, baby?" Thomasson said that he had heard this on the
television show *Kojak.* In all of the times Thomasson had lunged
towards me trying to kiss me, he had never uttered Kojak's
line. He was blatantly lying on the stand.

As far as Thomasson was concerned, I had misread everything done to me. He said that he had nipped at the fabric of
my leg in a "gotcha." Never had he pinched me on or near the

buttocks. As for headlocks, he had never and would never do anything like that. He felt that I had a lot of stress out there because I didn't know how to do my job. He and Hornbuckle had tried to help me with pointers, but I just couldn't seem to grasp it. In the end, he told the jurors, it didn't seem like I much cared about my job at all.

Steve was understandably upset when he began cross-examination. Thomasson was cocky on the stand with Beard, and his attitude continued with Steve. He denied ever physically assaulting me. He was very curt and had to be prodded to answer fully even the simplest of questions.

After Thomasson said he had no idea why I'd accuse him of anything, Steve asked him if I'd accused any of the other men on third shift besides Hornbuckle. Thomasson gave a pathetic, "I don't know."

Tom Burgay, the electrician from third shift, took the stand. He recited many of the same party lines. If Hornbuckle and Thomasson pinched me, it was all in good-natured fun. He felt that I was overly sensitive, and the defendants didn't mean anything by it. Besides, it looked to him like I didn't know how to take care of myself. Neither did I know how to do my job, he told the court. If I knew the job, I would have been able to reprimand my subordinates. As far as he could tell, I didn't really care about the job at all.

The last person to take the stand was Larry Hornbuckle. He gave the court background on his life until becoming a general foreman in Birmingham. He looked very uncomfortable and his eyes nervously looked around the room. Bulgarella asked Hornbuckle about the "can I see your dick?" question.

Apparently, it was all in good fun and had been used for years in Birmingham. No one had ever taken offense to the "colorful" saying. Hornbuckle admitted that he greeted me with those words, but that I was laughing and not in the least bit offended. *Here we go again*, I thought.

Next, Hornbuckle admitted to "goosing" me, but only on the back of the leg. He had never gotten anywhere near my buttocks. He told the court that I had never been hurt, offended, or asked him to stop.

Then, he laid out some more bald-faced lies. When Bulgarella asked him if he had ever used any offensive language directed towards Marcia, he sadly admitted that he had. However, he told the court, it was the same language that I used when describing my "women." To hear Hornbuckle tell it, I often referred to women as "cunts" in a bragging manner.

Then, Hornbuckle began telling the room about how incompetent I was on the job and how he and the others had tried to help me. It struck me that if I had been given as much help as the defense witnesses attested, I wouldn't have had much work to do. The way they told it, they practically held my hand during each shift. "I did everything I could to help him," said Hornbuckle.

Bulgarella asked Hornbuckle if he had treated me differently than any of the other employees. He said he had. Bulgarella wanted to know how had he treated me differently.

"Well, I just tried to take more time with him, be more patient and help him all I could."

When Steve cross-examined him, Hornbuckle played dumb. He had no idea why I would pick on him by charging him in a lawsuit. He imagined that it had to do with money. Furthermore, he had never done anything to me to warrant the charges. He was an innocent victim of my greed. Finally, Hornbuckle was through on the stand.

"Will there be rebuttal?" the judge asked Steve.

"No, sir, Your Honor," said Steve. "I think we have heard enough."

"That's one thing I think we can all agree on," said Judge Nelson.

Before adjourning for the night, McGivaren again tried to get the case thrown out. The judge seemed to be considering it. McGivaren argued that the evidence shown did not implicate the railroad in negligence.

The judge was reluctant, though, and felt that it should go

to the jury. Under the Federal Employment Liability Act, the wording was such that Norfolk Southern could be held responsible if representatives from the company contributed in the negligence. In my case, Hornbuckle could be considered a company representative.

Steve was pleased with the decision, but Judge Nelson had more to say.

"Well, I think that the evidence is pretty strong that Mr. Martin either knew, should have known, had the ability, had the means to do something, and he didn't do it," said the judge.

If he let the case go to the jury, he planned on telling them that "competent adults have an obligation to take care of themselves."

Even Judge Nelson seemed to side with the defense, albeit cautiously.

14

CLOSING ARGUMENTS

Birmingham, Alabama
June 11, 1996

My pride hung in the balance and I was literally sick to my stomach as the closing arguments were at hand. I felt that the defense team had done a pretty fair job of assassinating my character. Any person who had listened to the witnesses couldn't help but think that I was to blame. Steve told me not to worry. The best thing was to let the jury decide my case.

I reflected on the testimony given. Often, the most damaging statements were sandwiched between neutral statements. The defense knew what they were doing. Benson, Bishop, Thomasson, Burgay, and Hornbuckle all told the jury that they had nothing against me personally. They didn't feel one way or the other about me and only wanted to help me to do my job better.

Between these seemingly harmless statements, they slandered me with words like "incompetent," "easily stressed," and "too emotional."

I was suddenly struck with a realization. The defense witnesses, not including Hornbuckle and Thomasson, had absolutely no idea what I had been through. They couldn't possibly relate to what I was put through. No one could. It was one thing to hear about all of the terrible things in court testimony within a well-appointed courtroom. It was quite another to physically live them out in a dark, fog-filled railroad yard. So, besides wanting to keep their jobs with the railroad, these men had every reason to be good witnesses for the defense. They could not comprehend any of the charges I had brought. It was as foreign to them as flying through the air like Superman.

I had never felt so alone in all my life. I knew that I was going to lose and that people would laugh at me for the rest of my life. I began regretting even taking this mess to court. Who was I to take on a railroad? I was full of doubt – until Steve began his closing arguments.

"Most of the time, I'm on the defense side. I'm not a plaintiff's lawyer by trade, but that's not to say that some plaintiff's cases don't have merit. We think this one does," Steve told the jury.

He told the jury that the key to this case was my testimony and my credibility as a witness. It was their job to decide who were the more credible witnesses in this case. Steve pointed out that not once, since I had first told anyone of what had been done to me, had I changed my story. He asked the jurors not to be fooled by the defense attorneys when they said that we were adding to the original testimony. Steve went on:

"These lawyers questioned him for nine and a half hours. Much more stringently than they did on the stand here the other day, if you can believe it. And not once did they rattle him. They're saying all this stuff about, well, that's the first time I ever heard that. That's the first time I ever heard that. That's simply not true. That is simply not true. This testimony has been repeatedly testified about. The broom handle incident and all that stuff."

There was no surprise testimony on our part and the defense attorneys knew it.

Steve had a way of bringing out the important aspects of the case in the simplest ways. He was easy with the jury and didn't talk down to them. Whereas McGivaren and Beard were hostile during questioning and whenever they spoke, Steve spoke eloquently and calmly. He had a beautiful way of summing up hours of testimony in a few well-constructed sentences:

"I've played ball my whole life and been in a lot of locker rooms, and I've never seen the type of conduct that these people have described, that the witnesses have described. You know, they got up in opening statement the other day and they said it's going to be all of these peoples' testimony against Mr. Martin. They're trying to gang up on him in the courtroom just like they ganged up on him out there on third shift."

Steve asked the jury to award me lost wages, medical costs, and punitive damages. He said the amount of money that they awarded me for suffering would be up to them. We weren't in it for the money. He sat down, not once having looked at any crib sheets in his twenty minutes of speaking.

Beard went next. In his usual sarcastic tone and inflammatory nature, he attempted to rip apart Steve's arguments. He said that indeed, I was the key to the case. However, I was not to be trusted. Not once had I ever been responsible while I worked for the railroad. He brought up a letter of reprimand from eight years prior, he discussed my lack of assertiveness, and my family's history. In short, he attacked me again and again about things that had absolutely nothing to do with the charges.

"This man did not do his job. And when he came here to see you, he could not accept responsibility for it and tried to deflect it to other people who had nothing to do with it," Beard told the jurors.

Talk about calling the kettle black, I thought. The defense attorneys had done nothing but try to shift responsibility to anyone but their clients. Steve could have taken the exact statement and inserted "Norfolk Southern" in place of "this man." I could only half listen as Beard went on and on about my incompetence on the job and in life.

Much like Thomasson's behavior, nothing was out of bounds for Beard. As far as he was concerned, anything in my life was fair game. "You know, it was very interesting to me – and I've been doing this for about as long as Mr. Poer has – it was very interesting to me that the first discussion that you heard from Mr. Martin was about money. They don't even have him on the stand five minutes, and we've got to hear about all the money he made on the railroad and all the benefits that he had. That tells you what this case is about."

I couldn't believe the statement about "all the money" I'd been making on the railroad, as if I were some robber baron who burned hundred dollar bills to light cigars. Beard really knew how to pour salt on a wound. I wished I could have asked him how much he made each year defending people like Thomasson. I would wager it was a lot more than I would ever have seen at the railroad if I'd worked there for thirty years.

"And as to Mr. Thomasson, I would ask you to return a verdict in his favor and send him back to his family and send Mr. Martin back to his family. Let them get on with their life and get past this, because they have not met the burden of proof. You cannot trust Mr. Martin," Beard said in conclusion.

When I looked at Steve and Beverly, they weren't in the least bit rattled. They took notes while Beard spoke and weren't stung by any of the words he used. I wished that I could be as calm and unaffected as they were. It was difficult when the subject of everyone's speech was my life. Beverly gave me a reassuring smile.

Bulgarella spoke after Beard. It was more of the same for the jury, but he substituted Hornbuckle's name for Thomasson's. Bulgarella told the women and men on the jury that I had exaggerated in my charges and statements. All that I had been subjected to was good old-fashioned horseplay. I took things the wrong way. Besides, he said I had never received any psychological tests to determine if I was lying or not.

As far as he and his client were concerned, I had never asked Hornbuckle to stop "playing" around with me. Had I asked him to, he would have stopped immediately. His client was not responsible for any of my problems. In Bulgarella's estimation, it was the alcohol and prescription drugs that caused all of my symptoms. Conveniently, he didn't mention the fact that the reason I was taking prescription drugs was to alleviate the symptoms in the first place. He went on to say:

"I would ask you that when you consider whatever happened to Mr. Martin and whatever damage was caused by that, to consider the whole picture. Consider whether these damages and these problems were the result of some pinching and some words that were used, or . . . the results of several failed marriages, several nasty divorces; an inability to perform his job at a satisfactory level."

It was like a final jab when the fighter was on his way down, a final punch before the referee pulled the opponent away to his side of the ring. Nothing was out of bounds for the defense, especially not poor taste.

McGivaren was the last of defense counsel to offer closing arguments. I braced myself for his onslaught, which I knew would be the most inflammatory of the bunch. McGivaren had a way of twisting the knife in wounds he had previously inflicted. He greeted the jurors cordially and launched into his defense of Norfolk Southern:

"This case is about a young man who went from the minor leagues to the major leagues. And in going there, he took along a lot of baggage. And when he arrived and he put his bag down and he went to the plate, he found out that the game was the same. You play it on the same kind of field. You play it with the same equipment. You use – see the same kinds of plays, but it ain't the same. It's different. It's real different. And it wasn't long before he realized that it was very likely that he wasn't going to make it. He couldn't grasp it. The job was running him, he wasn't running the job."

McGivaren told the jurors that because I was in a supervisory position, I should have been able to handle all of the problems on my own. It was because of my own shortcomings, not Norfolk Southern's, that the problems persisted.

"When he got here and it came his turn to step up to bat," said McGivaren, "and it came his turn to be a member of a big league team and to do what it was he was getting paid to do, he didn't even take a turn at the plate."

I wouldn't have been surprised if the counselors for the defense had researched my family and knowingly told the jury that I came from dishonest stock because my great-great-grandfather had once cheated on his math homework. They were zealous in their attempts to ruin my name. They relished dishing out the alleged "dirt" on me and those close to me. During the trial, they had dragged in my ex-wife, my father, my sister, and, with more viciousness, Marcia. Both Marcia and Lynn had been forced to tears on the stand. I hoped, for all of our sakes, that the jury could sort through and sift out the garbage the defense had heaped on top of the facts.

Because the burden of proof was up to Steve, Beverly, and me, Steve was allowed a rebuttal to the defense counselors' closing arguments. I knew that he had done well on his first argument, but I didn't know if he would be able to answer all that was touched on. There were so many insults and accusations aimed at me, that it might take Steve a week to answer them all. He knew his job, though, and picked through their arguments and focused on specific remarks.

The jury was more attentive now than they had been during the entire trial. Perhaps it was because they were tired and wanted to go home, or perhaps it was because the closing arguments were almost dirtier than the testimony given. Whatever the reason, Steve had them on the edges of their seats.

With regard to McGivaren's baseball analogies, Poer rebutted, "This ain't no baseball game, first of all. This is real life. It's very serious to Mr. Martin."

Darn right, I thought. It was all that I could think about. Steve went on:

"But let's just take this baseball analogy out a little further. ... He goes up – his first time at bat, and he's got a disgruntled old pro on the other side that doesn't like the success that this young man has had. You know what he does? He throws the ball at his head . . . He hit him in the head when the boy was taking his turn at bat . . . They put him out of the game. That's what this case is all about."

Steve wasn't through with his fierce argument. He wasn't going to let McGivaren off that easy: ". . . they symbolically raped the man on his job. True. They didn't get undressed and they didn't do anything physical in that way to him, but they took his pride and they took his dignity. And he has the right to have both of those in his place of employment . . . And that's what we are here for today. It's not to make up any analogies about baseball games. It's not to ask for something we're not entitled to. This man's life has been ruined."

For the next few minutes, he went over the points of our case again. He told the jurors how to determine what my lost wages were. He told them how to arrive at punitive damages, but he restated that we were not asking for a specific amount. Whatever they felt I deserved, I would be satisfied with.

Steve's passionate discourse came straight from the heart. He didn't like to see the might of Norfolk Southern ganging up on me. He finished, "It's not the lost wages and all that, it's the mental well-being. It's your pride. It's your respect. It's your human dignity. That's what these people have taken away from this man. And we're asking you to return it to him."

I felt like standing up in my chair and cheering. I was truly touched and amazed that Steve had so clearly found the essence of my case. I knew that when I stopped on Beverly's name over two years earlier, someone up there was looking out for me. Both she and Steve were not typical attorneys. They genuinely cared about my well-being, and it showed in all that they did.

Before Judge Nelson gave the jury his instructions and left them to deliberate, he got word that one of the jurors was sick and asking to be excused. None of the attorneys objected to him being dismissed, but before the judge did that, he decided to talk to him. The juror felt that if he were allowed to go home for the rest of the day, he would feel better the next day. Because Judge Nelson wanted the entire jury to decide the case, he dismissed the jurors shortly after lunch for the rest of the day.

At nine the next morning, Judge Nelson was ready with his instructions for the entire jury. He began, "Now that you've heard all of the evidence and the arguments of the lawyers, I must explain to you the rules of law that you are required to follow and to apply in deciding the case. When I have finished, you will go back to the jury room and begin your deliberations."

I found it interesting that all of the attorneys were allowed to argue about the points that the judge would tell to the jurors in his instructions. If they didn't agree with a statement, they were given ample opportunities to tell the judge so. That was one of many aspects that you never saw on film. On television shows, the judge always dismissed the jury with a simple, "The jury will now deliberate on the case."

Judge Nelson spoke to the jury for over an hour before letting them go. His instructions were a summation of the case thus far. He summed up the list of my charges and how they were supposed to rule on them. He explained what the term "burden of proof" meant. He told them how to consider witness testimony and physical evidence.

There was also the matter of "stipulation of facts." These were facts that the parties, both plaintiff and defense, had agreed were true. He read them to the jury and provided them with a copy of all the facts.

When taking into account witness testimony, Judge Nelson told the jury that there were certain questions they might ask: Did the person impress you as one who was telling the truth? Did the witness have any particular reason not to tell the truth? Did the person have a personal interest in the outcome of the case? Did the witness seem to have a good memory? Did the witness have the ability and the opportunity to observe accurately the things that the witness testified about? Did the witness's testimony differ from other testimony or other evidence in the case?

They were all standard questions, but ones that needed to be stressed. Judge Nelson summed up my charges for the jurors:

"The plaintiff, Edwin Berry Martin, claims that after he was transferred by the Norfolk Southern Railway to its Norris Yard facility in November of 1993, the individual defendants engaged in a course of conduct while on the job to ridicule, humiliate him and embarrass him in that they continually and consistently made rude comments and lewd and obscene gestures to and about the plaintiff and subjected him to unprovoked and uninvited physical contact. Based upon these claims, Mr. Martin asserts that Norfolk Southern negligently failed in its duty to provide him with a reasonably safe workplace. He also claims that the individual defendants invaded his privacy, assaulted and battered him."

I couldn't have said it better myself.

If it seemed like he was going to be totally impartial, Judge Nelson made another statement to the jurors that seemed to target me. I hoped it wouldn't affect the outcome, but I later supposed it was a fair statement. He told the jury:

"The law places upon every competent adult person the duty to take reasonable steps to protect his own interests. These steps include the obligation for Mr. Martin to inform himself and take advantage of Norfolk Southern's policies and the procedures provided by it by which he might have obtained relief from the circumstances about which he now complains."

In other words, the jury had to take into account that I could have complained further up the chain of command before taking my claims to court. That had been one of Judge Nelson's problems with my case from the get-go. He reacted the way I imagined my father might. The judge thought that had I taken things into my own hands, I could have handled it more like a man. Again, I was struck by the idea that the judge had never been put in my situation. I doubted very much that Judge Nelson could calmly deal with men who were intent on seeing him suffer.

For the next forty-five minutes, he told the jury how to look at the evidence and how to award damages, if any. The jurors looked bored when he began discussing mathematical calculations and how to factor in inflation and rates. He was obligated to discuss the matters, though. Finally, he let the jurors go. My fate now truly rested in their hands.

15

JUST REWARDS

Birmingham, Alabama
June 12, 1996

I felt all the composure in my body seep out as the jury left to deliberate my case. Judge Nelson gave them extremely detailed instructions, so detailed that I feared for the jury's patience for the case during deliberations. As they retired to the jury room, the jurors took with them mounds of paperwork, both evidence and instructions.

I couldn't help but imagine the nine people sitting at the board table with a look of horror on their faces as they surveyed all the evidence that they were obligated to sort through. I couldn't imagine a worse fate than having to read through page after page of legal papers.

"Let's just forget the evidence," one of them might say. "I think this Eddie Martin guy is a phony. Let's just say 'not guilty' and go on home."

I shook my head to clear it and walked out of the courtroom. We waited almost the entire day before being called back. During lunch in the court's cafeteria, we pushed food around on our plates. No one was hungry. Steve and Beverly looked calm despite the tension. They had done all they could do and were satisfied that the jury heard enough evidence to find for me. Every worst-case scenario floated through my mind. I was happy to have Marcia with me. She kept me from screaming or weeping – and I felt like doing both.

While waiting for the jury, we tried to occupy our time. We weren't allowed to leave the courthouse and there weren't a whole lot of things to do to pass the hours. Marcia and I smoked many cigarettes. I cursed the habit and the dark day when I started. I hated the darn things, but they certainly served as a security blanket during those long hours.

When Steve told me it was time to go back into the court-room, my stomach was moving like a butter churn. I took deep breaths and tried to will myself to be calm. I didn't think the jury had convened for nearly long enough to arrive at their judgment. A quick decision was not a good sign for me. It took less time to say "not guilty" than "guilty." I began preparing for the bad news.

It was very bad news, but not at all what I expected. Beard rose and addressed Judge Nelson, "Judge, I was advised some-time this afternoon . . . my client and Mr. Hornbuckle had seen Mrs. Martin this afternoon conversing downstairs with two of the husbands of the jurors."

He went on to say that the day before, Marcia was observed "having some type of conversation" with a juror and her hus-band. In other words, he was accusing us of jury tampering, an extremely serious offense. It was serious enough to warrant the judge's undivided attention.

Beard had practiced nothing but underhanded techniques throughout the trial, and if I saw him choking, I'd think twice before helping him. Marcia was a friendly person by nature. She might say "hello" to anyone, but she would never tamper with a jury. We had too much to lose.

Steve said that if defense wanted to nitpick, he had person-ally seen one of the defense witnesses and Thomasson speak-ing well within earshot of all the jurors a couple days earlier. Thomasson complained about how badly he had been treated

and the fact that he had to defend this case. Steve told the
judge that he hadn't said anything earlier, but had found it
highly inappropriate. Judge Nelson was not a happy man.

"Let me say something to all of you: If we need to conduct
an investigation, I have the means to do that. The Special Agent
in Charge of the FBI in Birmingham, Alabama, is named Mr.
Lankford, and I have his telephone number. The sort of thing
that I have heard described, if it happened, might well be described in the criminal statutes as jury tampering, and people
go to jail for jury tampering."

Furthermore, he told us, if he needed to conduct an investigation, he was going to have to do it now, because he was
going to be elsewhere the next day. His colleague, Judge
Blackburn, would be available the next day to take a verdict.

Beard said that a hearing was not necessary, but he wanted
to ask Marcia some questions. For the first time in a long time,
I felt my blood boil in anger. I knew that Beard was not going
to be kind to my wife on the stand. I was right. He fired questions at her like a machine gun.

Beard: "Mrs. Martin, do you smoke cigarettes?"

Marcia: "Yes, I do."

Beard: "Have you had any occasion to smoke any cigarettes while you've been here?"

Marcia: "Yes, sir."

Beard: "And where is that done?"

Marcia: "Either outside the front of the building or outside
the back of the building."

He asked her if she had smoked that day, and if she'd seen
and spoken to two men whose wives were jurors. She told him
she had. They had asked her questions and she answered. She
remembered one man apologizing to her a week earlier for
speaking to her during the trial's beginning. Then, as if smell-
ing blood, Beard pounced on her.

"Well, when you say they might ask you a question, did
they ask you a question this week or did they not ask you a

question this week?" asked Beard.

"I think they asked me if the jury was on a break or something like that, or if it was raining—"

"You think or do you know?" interrupted Beard. "I'm asking about this week."

And on it went. Beard exhibited a viciousness unseen during the trial. He was unrelenting and harsh. Marcia was scared, and it showed in her voice and mannerisms.

I hated him for what he was doing. First, he had taunted me during Thomasson's investigation, pretending that I had told him I was going to "break his neck." Then, he had attempted to humiliate my sister, wife, and me on the stand. Now, he was attacking Marcia again. It seemed that he and Thomasson were cut from the same mold.

Marcia explained that she had not spoken to anyone; they had spoken to her. If they asked her a simple question, such as "is the jury on break?" she would nod her head. She remembered that Steve had explained to her that she was not allowed to speak to anyone having anything to do with the jury during the trial. However, she couldn't help it if she was outside smoking a cigarette when jurors' husbands came over to her.

Marcia was on the verge of tears, and at one point the judge told Beard, "I really don't think that it's necessary to be quite so overbearing."

Beard didn't seem to hear him and kept questioning Marcia. He asked her about the conversations she had with a clerk of the court. He asked her how long she spent outside. He asked her about any contact she'd had with the defendants.

It was a witch-hunt, and for the first time I realized that Beard was scared. If he had felt comfortable about the trial, there was no way he would trump up these charges.

Finally, Judge Nelson had heard enough. Steve asked her flat-out if she had attempted to communicate with any of the jurors. She told him she hadn't. She also stated that she hadn't tried to influence anybody's decision in the trial.

"Mrs. Martin," began Judge Nelson, "out of an abundance of caution, I think it might be well when you leave the courthouse this afternoon that you not come back until after the jury has returned a verdict in this case."

"Okay," she said, her eyes catching mine. "Yes, sir."

My heart sank. I needed her by my side when the verdict was read. She made me feel safe when things were at their darkest. My head was spinning in so many directions that I had absolutely no inkling as to which way the jury would swing. It could go either way. Whatever they decided, I wanted my wife holding my hand when this thing was all over.

❖   ❖

We got to the courthouse early the next morning. The jury had still not reached a verdict, and I was as anxious as a death row inmate on hanging day. Sitting in place of Judge Nelson was Judge Sharon L. Blackburn. Judge Nelson was out of town for some conferences. I would rather have finished the trial with the same judge we had started with, but at this point it made no difference. Others didn't see it that way.

Beard moved for a mistrial because of alleged jury tampering. Judge Blackburn was caught off guard. Obviously, she said, she wanted to talk to Judge Nelson about it. She heard the details of Marcia's alleged tampering, then said she would call Judge Nelson. Before she did, both Bulgarella and Graham joined in on the motion for Hornbuckle and Norfolk Southern, respectively.

As she was about to call, a juror knocked on the door from the jury room. Beard wanted the record to show that he had made his motion before the knock. The clerk approached the bench with a note from the jury. The note read: "Judge, we cannot agree" and was signed by the foreperson.

Judge Blackburn commented that she now had two things to discuss with Judge Nelson. When Steve asked her if he needed to respond to the motion, she told him that she didn't think so, because Judge Nelson would probably not grant it.

Before she called Judge Nelson, and in lieu of the jury note, she asked the attorneys how they felt about her giving them an "Allen charge." Steve wanted one, and the other lawyers didn't object if the motion for mistrial were rejected.

An Allen charge is a term used to identify the instructions given to a jury when it fails to reach a verdict. Usually, the judge will speak with the jurors about the importance of their reaching a verdict. The judge might reiterate to them that they are the ones who have heard all the evidence and are in the best position to decide on the case.

Judge Blackburn talked with Judge Nelson and, as she expected, he did not grant a mistrial. She read us the proposed Allen charge and there were no objections to any of the language. Then, she convened the jury and read them her instructions. It was a precise and logical statement. She ended the charge with: "You may be as leisurely in your deliberations as the occasion may require and should take all the time you feel is necessary." The jury left again to continue their deliberations.

Shortly after 10 A.M., Judge Nelson called and wanted a conference call with the attorneys.

"I understand your jury is having some problems," he said.

"Yes, sir, apparently so," replied Steve.

He then asked if we were interested in settling the lawsuit right then and there. Steve told him that we were always interested in talking, but that it seemed like the two sides were at great distances from each other on what they wanted.

Judge Nelson was adamant on not trying the case again. None of us wanted to try it again. Judge Nelson asked Steve the "money" question next: how much did I want? Steve told the judge he hadn't discussed it with me, but felt I should get at least $200,000.

Judge Nelson answered, "I think that's ludicrous, just to give you a straight opinion. I don't think this lawsuit is worth that kind of money."

The judge suggested that we take Norfolk Southern's offer of $75,000, which McGivaren assured the room was still on the table. Steve said that he didn't feel that was enough after working on the case for over two years. Judge Nelson thought it was a fair settlement, especially since he felt we hadn't really proved our case. Steve said he'd talk to me about it, but still didn't feel comfortable with $75,000.

"If the jury eventually comes in with a verdict for the defendant, you don't get anything out of it," volunteered the judge.

"Yes, sir," said Steve politely. "I understand that, Judge."

"There is a time to cut bait and go," warned Judge Nelson.

"I understand, Judge," Steve told him. "I will talk to Mr. Martin about it."

Steve and I decided to wait on a jury's verdict. He didn't have to explain the consequences to me. I felt the same way that he did. We had been consumed by this case for over two years. I'd be damned before I let Norfolk Southern weasel their way out of it with pennies. They deserved to pay for what they allowed to happen to me. Norfolk Southern needed to experience pain. Hopefully, Hornbuckle and Thomasson would share in that pain.

I tried to hold my anger in check as I glanced over at the defendants' table. Hornbuckle was cutting up with his lawyers and Thomasson. The attorneys looked relaxed and read newspapers. They made me sick. None of them seemed in the least bit worried. Their arrogance knew no boundaries, and I prayed that they'd be made to pay.

I walked out of the courtroom and down to a bench in the courthouse lobby. I needed badly to clear my head and massaged my temples while staring at the floor. Perhaps it was my facial expression. Perhaps my silent prayers reached someone. I looked up from the floor into the eyes of an elderly black woman. She looked to be in her nineties, and her skin was weathered and lined. Everything about her told of struggles and hardships – everything except her eyes. The woman's eyes were a deep green and danced with youth.

She didn't say a word to me as she approached. As she neared me, she reached out her hands and I took hold of her thin fingers. Her face arched up to the heavens and she prayed for God to look out for me. I dared not speak a word. After a couple minutes of prayer, she gave my hands a gentle squeeze and released them. Then, with a soft smile, she turned and walked away. I went back to the courtroom a new man.

❖   ❖

The jury reached a verdict at 11:10 A.M. The moment of truth was upon me. They could find for the defendants and I would get less than nothing – my pride and any hopes I had of putting this mess behind me would be lost. They could find for me and award me $1.00. I'd heard of that happening, and the idea scared me.

"I understand the jury has reached a verdict," said Judge Blackburn.

"Yes, they have," said the foreperson.

"Has the jury reached a verdict on all claims – with regard to all the claims in the case?"

"Yes, we have."

"Is your verdict a unanimous verdict of all the jurors?" asked the judge.

"Yes, ma'am," the foreperson answered.

As the clerk read the verdict, I concentrated on the words that flowed from his mouth. The first charges to be answered were under FELA against Norfolk Southern. The question for the jury was, "Do you find from a preponderance of the evidence that the defendant Norfolk Southern was negligent in the manner claimed by the plaintiff and that such negligence was a legal cause of damage to the plaintiff?"

There was an eternity between the reading of the charge question and the jury's verdict.

"Yes."

I wanted to cheer. I wanted to cry. Somehow, I held myself together. There were other charges I needed to hear. Because the jury answered "yes," they needed also to answer whether they felt I, too, was negligent. They answered "yes."

My heart sank. The next question dealt with awarding percentages of negligence to each party. There was a drum roll in my head and heart.

"Norfolk Southern, 75 percent; Edwin Berry Martin, 25 percent."

I could live with that. I didn't necessarily agree with it, but I certainly could live with the verdict. To me, it meant that Norfolk Southern was three times more guilty of negligence than I was. The jury obviously felt that I could have done more to prevent it. Funny, that was the same question I had for myself when Hornbuckle and Thomasson were harassing me.

The biggest surprise came with the next charge question. Without factoring in the percentages of guilt, what amount did the jury feel should be awarded for the negligence?

The jury must have been anxious to leave, because they answered with a number no one was expecting: $500,000. That meant that I would receive seventy-five percent of that sum, or $375,000. I felt dizzy and set a hand on the table in front of me to steady myself.

Then came the charges against Thomasson. With regard to assault and battery, they found him not guilty. With regard to invasion of privacy, they found him guilty. However, they awarded me no compensatory damages and only $100 in punitive damages. Thomasson was getting off with a slap on the wrist. The jury probably believed that because he was my subordinate, he wasn't as liable. Their verdict stung, but I didn't let it get to me. He would be judged by a higher power.

Last, the charges against Hornbuckle were read. Again, they

found for the defendant regarding assault and battery. I felt my face getting red as I imagined Hornbuckle sneering and bobbing his head to the verdict. They found for me on the invasion of privacy charge. I waited to hear if Hornbuckle would get a simple slap on the wrist like Thomasson had.

The jury again awarded no compensatory damages. They didn't let him off as easily as his partner, though. They fined him $2,500 in punitive damages. Hornbuckle, with his fine and attorney costs, would have to pay.

The trial ended shortly thereafter. When all was said and done, I shook Steve's hand and hugged Beverly tightly. They had done the impossible for me. The congratulations and smiles felt great, but they were bittersweet. There was a person missing from our quartet, and I knew she was at the law offices waiting for me. I couldn't wait to get there.

On our way out of the courtroom, McGivaren came up to me and said, "Don't spend that money, yet. It ain't over."

I kept my mouth shut, which was hard to do. I wouldn't give him the satisfaction of a response. I had heard enough from him: nine and a half hours in a deposition and an hour and a half on the witness stand. If he had anything left to say, he could tell it to Steve or Beverly.

When we got to the law offices, the staff gave me a round of applause. Steve said a quick good-bye to me and I tried to thank him. I couldn't find the words. He assured me that there would be appeals and motions and all manner of other tactics employed by McGivaren and company. He also assured me that, in the end, I would see a check for over $300,000. Then, he turned on his heel and left for Atlanta.

Beverly was easier to thank. She was the reason I was celebrating. I hugged her again and thanked her for all of her work. She was glad that the good guys won. We both agreed that we were happy it was finally over.

I hugged Marcia tightly. She, of course, had heard the news before we arrived. Marcia had been with me from the start.

Now, she was there to help me celebrate its passing. I had finally beaten the giant, Marcia holding my hand through it all. Whenever I had faltered, she picked me up and made me go on. I loved her more than I could ever express.

After months of sadistic abuse, after two and a half years of waiting, and after two weeks of lies, tears, and dirt in a courtroom, I was finally ready to go home.

16

EPILOGUE

South Carolina
Present Day

I am haunted by the memories. As I hear the far-off cry of a train, I am reminded of my ordeal. Every time I look into a mirror and remember the gaunt, tormented face that once stared back at me, I think of Birmingham. I will never shake the nightmares, no matter how long I am in therapy. Nor, for some reason, would I want to. What happened to me, helped make me a stronger man than I ever was. It forced me to face my fears head on and overcome them.

Norfolk Southern finally paid off, over a year after the trial ended. We even told Norfolk Southern that we'd accept $25,000 less than what the jury awarded in order to speed up the process. McGivaren did as Steve said he would. He hemmed and hawed until he couldn't any longer. Steve made him see that. McGivaren knew he was lucky when Judge Nelson had thrown out the sexual harassment charge before trial for fear it would be overturned on appeal. However, when the Supreme Court ruled on March 4, 1998, that men could sexually harass other men, Steve pointed this out to the railroad attorney.

Steve's letter to McGivaren read simply, "In view of the

Supreme Court's ruling today . . . I have been instructed by my client to withdraw our offer of $350,000 to settle this matter if not accepted within fourteen (14) days of this letter."

As Steve expected, Norfolk Southern promptly paid up – and shut up. My dealings with my grandfathers' and fathers' railroad company came to an end.

Marcia and I again live a full and healthy life. I am no longer afraid of crowds or venturing outdoors. We live in the house that I built with my own two hands. I see my children whenever I can. The sounds and sights of nature once again captivate me. I slow-cook slabs of ribs on the barbecue while my kids run around with the dogs.

I appreciate all that I have with a newfound sense of what is important. For a while there, I thought that the railroad was the only thing that mattered. I was wrong. It is all that life has to offer – the ups, downs, triumphs, and defeats – that really matters. I celebrate life. I breathe it fully into my lungs as if each breath were my last.

Though I am still seeing Dr. Robbins for counseling, I find that I need her less and less with each visit. Sometimes I'll go a couple weeks without feeling any stress whatsoever. It is nice to know that she is there whenever Marcia and I might need her, though. She has been our guide to understanding and our friend when we needed one.

I have just completed training as a real estate appraiser, and it feels funny to be starting a brand new field when friends my age are nearing the halfway point in their chosen professions. This year would mark my nineteenth year with the railroad if I hadn't encountered the stuff nightmares are made of. Then again, I might still be living each day for the railroad, never knowing what other dishes life had to offer.

Marcia and I are blissfully happy. She has made the house I built into a home by giving it what it always lacked: love. On weekdays, she runs her own successful small business. On nights and weekends, we celebrate each and every hour together. It doesn't really matter if we go out of town or take a quiet walk down the street. With Marcia, everything is special.

Despite the horrors I faced on the railroad and at the hands of railroad men, I still hold a special place in my heart for trains. At one point, during my darkest hour, I thought that I would forever hate the machines. But how can I? The hundred speeding tons of steel and steam rushing down a sand-blasted rail are still in my blood. The awesome power of the engines as they pull millions of pounds of cargo behind them still captivates me. I still get nostalgic when I hear the lonely whistle of a far-off locomotive, and I imagine myself as a child running alongside and waving at my father until the train disappears down the track and out of sight.

Although I'm still a railroad lover, I'm no longer a railroad man. But in the process of being brutally severed from that generations-long bond to my family's history, I hope that I helped set an example for other victims of sexual harassment. Now the law is clear: there is no difference between same-sex and opposite-sex sexual harassment in the workplace. They are both reprehensible and unacceptable by any standard of human decency. But now, in addition, both are equally and officially illegal in the eye of the law.

APPENDIX

SOURCES OF SUPPORT AND INFORMATION ON SEXUAL HARASSMENT

The following organizations provide help to both men and women. Many more support groups exist for female survivors of sexual abuse. The list is divided into three sections: organizations and support groups for victims of sexual harassment; Internet sites and services concerning sexual harassment; and books that define and describe sexual harassment and what to do about it.

Organizations and Support Groups

American Psychological Association
750 1st Street, NE
Washington DC 20002
Telephone: (202) 336-5500

Type of support: Referrals to state and local associations that provide specialists who deal with psychological problems associated with sexual harassment. Publish pamphlets on how to choose a therapist.

Center for Working Life
3814 SE Martins Street
Portland OR 97202
Telephone: (503) 774-6088

Type of support: Provides workshops and training in the

workplace as well as support groups for those who have been sexually harassed.

Discrimination and Sexual Harassment Support Group (D.A.S.H.)

P.O. Box 7972
Boulder CO 80306
Telephone: (303) 441-5992

Type of support: D.A.S.H. offers telephone counseling, moral support and strategies for resolution, legal advice, attorney and therapist referrals, and a monthly support group in the Boulder, Colorado, area.

Equal Employment Opportunity Commission (EEOC)

1801 L Street, N.W.
Washington DC 20507 USA
Telephone: (202) 663-4900
TDD: (202) 663-4494
WWW home page: http://www.eeoc.gov/

To be automatically connected with the nearest EEOC field office:

Telephone: (800) 669-4000
TDD: (800) 669-6820

Type of support: The EEOC has the latest information on laws prohibiting job discrimination and how employees can file charges of employment discrimination, including sexual harassment. You must file a complaint with the EEOC before bringing a legal action in court. All information is presented in both English and Spanish.

Equal Rights Advocates
> 1663 Mission Street, Suite 550
> San Francisco CA 94103
> Telephone: (415) 621-0672
> 24-hour Hotline: (415) 621-0505
> Toll Free: (800) 839-4372
> Email: eradvocates@earthlink.net

Type of support: Legal advice and counseling in both English and Spanish.

Legal Aid Society, Employment Law Center, Workers' Rights Hotline
> Hastings Law School
> 1663 Mission Street, Suite 400
> San Francisco CA 94103
> Telephone: (415) 864-8848
> Workers' Rights Hotline: (415) 864-8208

Type of support: Free legal advice to poor and unemployed people and legal referrals.

National Employment Lawyers Association (NELA)
> 535 Pacific Avenue
> San Francisco CA 94134
> Telephone: (415) 227-4655
> Or (212) 603-6491 (New York City only)

Type of support: NELA maintains a national attorney network; they will refer you to a NELA member in your area if you send them a self-addressed, stamped envelope.

National Job Problem Hotline
Toll free: (800) 522-0925

The National Organization on Male Sexual Victimization (NOMSV) and Men, Assisting, Leading & Education (MALE)
PMB 103
5505 Connecticut Avenue, NW
Washington DC 20015-2601
Telephone: (800) 738-4181
URL: http://www.malesurvivor.org/
Email: info@malesurvivor.org

Type of support: Both organizations work to prevent, treat and end the sexual victimization of boys and men. They provide information and advocacy to victims.

National Victim Center
Telephone: (703) 276-2880
Toll free: (800) FYI-CALL (394-2255)

Pro Bono Advocates
CL88
50 West Washington
Chicago IL 60602
Telephone: (312) 629-6945

Type of support: Referrals to attorneys or legal agencies.

Rape Victim Advocacy Program (RVAP)
24-hour Hotline: (800) 284-7821
URL: http://www.uiowa.edu/rvap.html

Type of support: Support, information, advocacy and referrals for male and female victims of any kind of sexual abuse.

S.A.V.E.S.
P.O. Box 349
Farmington ME 04938
Telephone: (207) 778-9522
Hotline: (800) 221-9191

Type of support: Legal advocacy and referrals, training programs for businesses, local support groups.

Survivors of Sexual Crimes, Inc.
P.O. Box 2324
Hot Springs AR 71914
24-hour Hotline: (502) 624-7788

Type of support: Psychologist and psychiatrist referrals, counseling and self-help support group.

Trial Lawyers for Public Justice
1625 Massachusetts Avenue NW, Suite 100
Washington DC 20036
Telephone: (202) 797-8600

Type of support: Provide lawyers who take sexual harassment cases, some on contingency or sliding scale fees.

Internet Sites and Services

AWG- Sexual Harassment Paper, "Sexual Harassment: How to Recognize It . . . What to Do About It." J. E. Tagudin.
URL http://www.awg.org/docs/harass.html

FMF-Sexual Harassment Hotline Resource List:
URL http://www.feminist.org/911/harass.html

Male Abuse Survivors Support Forum:
URL http://www.noahgrey.com/massf/

Sexual Harassment – frequencies by gender:
URL http://www.vix.com/pub/men/harass/studies/larsen.html/

Sexual Harassment – What to Do When Harassed:
URL http://www.feminist.org/911/harasswhatdo.html/

Stop Sexual Harassment – "Have You Ever Been Upset By Unwanted Sexual Behavior Or Comments At Work?"
URL http://www.resources.org/

Books

Bernbach, Jeffrey M. *Job Discrimination II: How to Fight, How to Win.* Voire Dire Press, 1998.

Bravo, Ellen and Ellen Cassedy. *The 9 to 5 Guide to Combating Sexual Harassment: Candid Advice from 9 to 5, the National Association of Working Women.* John Wiley & Sons, Inc., 1992.

Callender, Dale. *Sexual Harassment Claims: Step-By-Step* (Legal-Ease Series). Barron's Educational Series, 1998.

Eisaguirre, Lynn. *Sexual Harassment: A Reference Handbook* (Contemporary World Issues Series). 2nd Edition. ABC-Clio, 1997.

Eskenazi, Martin, David Gallen and Michele A. Palud. *Sexual Harssment: Know Your Rights!* Carroll & Graf, 1992.

Langelan, Martha J. and Catherine A. MacKinnon. *Back Off!: How to Confront and Stop Sexual Harassment and Harassers.* Simon & Schuster, 1993.

O'Shea, Tracy and Jane Lalonde. *Sexual Harassment: A Practical Guide to the Law, Your Rights, and Your Options for Taking Action.* St. Martin's Press, 1998.

Petrocelli, William and Barbara Kate Repa. *Sexual Harassment on the Job: What It Is & How to Stop It.* 4th Edition. Nolo Press, 1999.

Webb, Susan L. *Step Forward: Sexual Harassment in the Workplace: What You Need to Know!* Master Media, 1998.

Write your own book review!

We love to hear from our readers, and we pass along all the reviews to the author. Tell us what you liked. Tell us what moved you. Tell us what you found most provocative!
Send your reviews to Corinthian Books, P.O. Box 1898, Mt. Pleasant, SC 29465 USA or e-mail them to:
reviews@corinthianbooks.com.
Thank you!